Nice Is Not Enough

Nice Is Not Enough!

Strategies To Develop Your Customer Server

Jeffrey L. Staton

SANKOFA HOSPITALITY LLC

Sankofa Publishing

Lumberton * North Carolina

Table Of Contents

Dedication

To Kalei "Lady" Marie Staton

My Loves

I love to see the big white moon,
A-shining in the sky
I love to see the little stars,
When the shadow clouds go by.

I love the rain drops falling
On my roof-top at night;

I love the soft wind's sighing,
Before the dawn's gray light

I love the deepness of the blue,
In my Lord's heaven above;
But better than all the things I think,
I love my LADY love.

-Langston Hughes

Introduction

$\mathcal{A}$t first glance, I know I look like your ordinary, hot middle-aged guy, similar to the male actors/models you see on commercials for erectile dysfunction. I'm just a hotelier, managing hotels across this great nation for over two decades. It wasn't my profession of choice. As a kid there was a tug-of-war between my desires to be a minister or a comedian. (Nowadays, I struggle to see the distinction. I could have totally done both simultaneously.)

The hospitality industry was a career of necessity. In college, I couldn't quite balance my efforts at being Casanova with my lesser efforts at being Dubois. Shaw University consequentially requested that I pursue a degree in other disciplines like life and not being there anymore - a request that dictated a decision: go back home or stay and work.

Well, I chose the latter, jumping head first into the sometimes tumultuous waters of the service industry and customer service.

At this point in my life, I cannot honestly say that my desire to be a comedic holy man has been lost in my role as hotel manager. Strangely enough there has been a time when a melding of the two was necessary. Like an army knife, I've had to whip out one or both of them to #1 stay sane; and, #2 to develop the brand of customer service I had to deliver in order to be successful in the hospitality industry. Countless emotionally explosive disasters have been diverted with a perfectly well-placed joke. (SN: self-deprecating humor does wonders. Customers love it when we imply we are idiots.) Also, I am unable to express how drawing strength from Biblical scriptures have enabled me to stay employed. Many days I thought: "Ok, Job lost his farm, his wife, and his sons. He stayed cool. This guy is only yelling, threatening me, and calling me liar. I think I can make it." I've spent many mornings driving to work wondering who I will be today, Billy Graham or Eddie Murphy.

The necessity to swing like a pendulum between those two personalities has shaped my personality, the way I interact with people outside of work, the type of friends I choose, the type of people I'm comfortable around. Most importantly, it has given me what I like to call the "Heart of A Real Servant." My stomach tightens every time I type or say the word "servant." It has attached to it, unfortunately, a densely negative connotation. As an African-American the consternation concerning the word is palatable. I am struck with sudden arthritis when I try to type the word, and stuttering issues when I try to say it. A Servant is definitely someone no one wants to be. Ironically, though, I'm tickled pink about being one. (SN: As a black dude, being tickled PINK should speak to the level at which I'm tinkled.) It is a badge of honor for me. I truly think serving is a natural fit for me. I'm not a big fan of mysticism; but, if I was I would say quite confidently that serving and I are meant to be together. It was written in the stars. Believe me. I should know. I have had clear view of stars circling my head after a long day of serving in my day.

Serving is perfect for me. I've never been the type of person that likes the lime light or being in the forefront of anything. It has always been immensely satisfying to know I'm the engine under the hood. Let someone else look good; let someone else get the attention. But, everyone including the heavenly host knows you can't go anywhere without me. That mindset is perfect for a real servant. The servant lowers him or herself to pick up someone. The servant bears the weight of the person they are lifting. Take away the servant, it all falls. Success is predicated upon my strength, my pain tolerance, my nerves, me – quiet, unheard, unseen, insignificant me. (Cue: the evil laugh)

Plus, and less maniacal sounding, I enjoy helping others achieve their goals, their wants. I find comfort in my life to know that because of me, someone achieved some semblance of level change.

Prior to me they were "here" emotionally, physically, whatever. Now from my direct input they have risen to "here," an increased level of understanding or an elevated position. That's awesome to me. There's no such thing as true altruism in this world. We get something out of everything that we do.

I've become quite good at being a servant. Once again I am attempting to cause level change in you by writing this book. We will take an exhaustively concise look at what it is to be a Customer Server and how to be one. My mission honestly is to cause a revolution—a servant revolution, certainly not a servant revolution in the likeness of the falling of the Bastille; but, hopefully equally as beneficial and resounding. The revolt I want to ignite should be resounding and hypnotizing, similar to the water bottling industry. The water bottling industry's witches and warlocks have convinced us TO BUY WATER! I want the revolt to be hypnotizing like the great Starbucks revolt. There are people right now buying $5.00 cups of coffee daily, several times a day. It is in this spirit I would love to see businesses demanding the best customer service and servers that nature can muster. It is my vision to see business owners no longer hiring customer service agents based upon simple, flimsy premises: they are cute, they speak well, they are nice, and they are loyal. I want to see department heads and owners hire more strategically, taking in to consideration the product they are selling, the physical locations, their type of clientele, the best and fitting personality type that will serve the aforementioned metrics.

Finally, I want to see customers demand better treatment. Awful and mediocre customer service has lulled our patrons to sleep. Their brains are torpid. They don't notice, except in extreme situations, that they are being mistreated. Our customers have accepted it and stopped demanding better. When the customers start wielding their power of the vote, their power to exact change through the all mighty dollar, patronizing only places that treat them wonderfully, taking their business only to stores, call centers, and buying products that understand the importance of their customer's experiences, being nice will become niche. Providing memorable, genuine customer service will be like the bottled water industry and Starbucks, a huge inextricable part of our culture.

"Nice Is Not Enough" will put you on the right side of the revolt. If implemented, this book will place you in a position of reception like a catcher behind the batter, ready to capture the onslaught of patrons, filling your grocery store isles, filling your phone banks, filling your pockets with wealth beyond imagining. While other CX books takes a needed examination of the patron in order to create the best customer service, "Nice Is Not Enough" looks at the service industry from the Server's, the engine under the hood's vantage point. Hire the appropriate customer server, you've accomplished, I believe a good chunk, of customer service.

It is my hope that you enjoy this instructional manual, that you will use it as a guide to correct your CX ills. I hope it gives you a different insight on how to run the business with in the business, the facilitation of your customers' needs and their precious experiences. As a Customer Server, we have tremendous power. As an owner, department head, team leader you have equally as much power, the power of setting the precedence, establishing a culture, styling a business that will seem attractive to anyone that sees it. It starts with executives knowing their product, being aware of their market, knowing the type of people that is best fit to display, to serve your product or service. It's your baby. Don't let just anyone be involved in something you've created with your sweat, with your time, with your money. It is my hope that his book will cause you to take another look at your business and critique honestly if you are providing the best CX possible. Is your success stagnated by your team? Are your servants too weak to hold you up? Do they have very feeble pain tolerances? Is the engine under your hood not working properly? This book will answer those questions for you. Let it teach you. Let it inspire you. Because, Nice Is Not Enough!

Chapter 1

Why do customers leave a company?

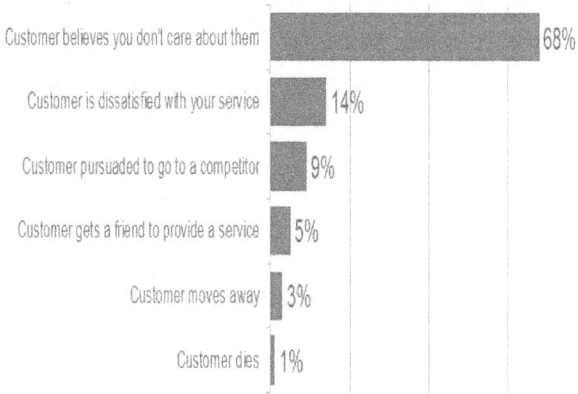

Customer believes you don't care about them	68%
Customer is dissatisfied with your service	14%
Customer pursuaded to go to a competitor	9%
Customer gets a friend to provide a service	5%
Customer moves away	3%
Customer dies	1%

Study by the Rockefellar Corporation

Grand Opportunity

ustomer services (CX) is one of those terms that has a definition that is illusive, similar to the el chupacarbra or Big Foot. I will give you my definition, sort of the angle at which I pursue CX. Cx, in my opinion, is best described as a grand opportunity. Each customer that walks into your store presents a grand opportunity to prove who and what you are. You say you produce an elite product, that your product excels above all others. You say your service produces the greatest utility and satisfaction. Well, each customer offers a grand opportunity to prove these premises. I remember starting my business. It was easier to find a snow ball in Texas than it was to find someone that would give me the opportunity to prove myself. All I wanted was an opportunity to show someone that I was the perfect choice for them; and that, bringing me aboard was the best idea that they could make. "Just give me a chance," I thought. It is in this light that you should view your Cx, as a precious chance – a chance to make a new convert, to proselytize, to swoon. View each customer encounter as an audition. You are not just auditioning for a simple role in a commercial, but for a serious part in a block buster movie. If awarded the role, your life will change profoundly. When that customer presents themselves to you…ACTION! You're On! Like a peacock displaying its marvelous kaleidoscopic plume, you unabashedly present yourself, your product, and your Customer Server to attract your desired patron in the direction of your business and away from other suitors.

I purposely labeled the opportunity "grand." The word "Grand" speaks to the treasured element or component that should be perceived in the opportunity. The moments when you have a customer's attention are hallowed moments. It is the universe opening up and allowing you to do and be what you've dreamed to be. How long have you wanted to be what you are? When you were getting your business off the ground, I'm sure you imagined the days when crowds of people would request your product or service; visions of people enjoying your talent was fondly imagined during the day and they provided comfort for you as you went to sleep at night. Back in the day, the concept of Customers held more profound connotations for you and your life. Recall the days when the sight of a customer entering your store would cause you to behave like a pet greeting its owner at the door after hours of work, how you would run to meet and greet them like children sprinting after the ice cream man. Remember those days? Where did they go? Somewhere in the process of building your "flower garden" you've become hypnotized by the beautiful scent and have forgotten that it is the flowers providing the wonderfully fragrant environment. The upkeep and maintenance of the flowers is paramount. Your customers are your flowers. They are affording you with an incredibly precious moment in life. In each customer lie your child's college education, your new home, your college loan payments, and many other Grand opportunities. The second that your day of serving customers become mundane and annoying is the day you've lost your vision. Create worth in your customer. Customers are not something you want. They are something you gotta have. Tony Robbins once said: "In life, we don't always get what we want. But, we always get what we gotta have." Les Brown once asked: "What is your "Why?" When you customers become your "Why," the fullness of the "grand" nature that is being presented to you by your customers will become unavoidably obvious and understood.

Cx is also a grand opportunity to express how thankful you are. It goes without saying that your product is "the best." Truth be told, your competition is singing the same "I'm The Best" tune. Here's a song that they are unable to sing, here's what you have that the others don't: THAT CUSTOMER, the one perusing your isles, the one presently on the phone, the one staring you in the face. They walked into your doors; they logged in to your website; they called you. You should, in turn, show your customers just how thankful you are by displaying the most incredible CX you can. The height, breadth, and length you are willing to display your Cx also indicates just thankful you are.

There are 3 ways to demonstrate your appreciation:

1. **Facial Expression.** Can you think of items that you have received of pivotal value (a gift, an offer, a visitation) that you have not emotionally expressed your appreciation? Scientist that study facial expression has learned that most people do not attribute the facial expression to being a depiction of what is happening internally or personally. They attribute your expression to being a reaction or response to them. In other words, when a customer walks in to your restaurant, the customer does not take in to consideration your day as a whole, they interpret your expression, as they encounter you, as a direct response to their presence.

In "The Emotional Contagion," an article written for Cambridge University in 1996, Elaine Hatfield described that, although she and her colleague were close friends, she could not avoid the feeling of inadequacy while having a conversation with her beloved friend. "I came away from the conversation feeling I said something stupid or bored him." She wrote. It wasn't until she discontinued analyzing her friend's mannerisms in the light of her own thoughts and feelings that she realized that her colleague's expression of "anxiety…twitching…and shifting weight from foot to foot" were often responses to her own countenances.

Listen, customers take your facial demeanor personally. In their minds, your countenance explains how you feel about them. To your customers your day just started when they arrived. It is easy for them to misinterpret your deadpanned reception as anger in response to their arrival, when in actuality that assessment is far from the truth. Don't underestimate the weight of facial expression. Appreciation is visible—as it should be. Your customers deserve to see your appreciation in your face.

2. **Your words.** Appreciation is visible. It is also vocal. You should literally mention how

thankful you are to your customer. In my days as a front desk agent, I would literally say: "I know you had other choices of hotels;" or I would say: "I know you passed several hotels on your way to us." Then I would thank them. Amy Moran, a psychotherapist, sought-after speaker, and author wrote an article for Forbes.com called "The Seven Scientifically Proven Benefits Of Gratitude That Will Motivate You To Give Thanks Year-Round." Number one of the seven was that gratitude opens doors for new relationships. She wrote: "…thanking a new acquaintance makes them more likely to seek ongoing relationships." She wrote: "acknowledging other people's contributions can lead to new relationships." As a business owner, does the words "new relationships" make you salivate? You can easily achieve this simply by saying thank you.

Human are what I like to call "Sound Beings." It doesn't matter what side of the isle you stand as it relates to the creation of the universe, whether you believe there was a "Big Bang!" that spawned creation or if you believe an Absolute Being spoke the world in existence. Either way, it is unmistakable that sound was involved. We were created by sound, so it stands to reason that we are affected by sound (words) be it negatively or positively. Sound is the essence of what we are.

What is that emanating from your earbuds while you are working out, that elevates your heartbeat that motivates you to lift heavier weights, run farther distances, to do what you would not do if you didn't have your earbuds on? Sound. What is that emanating from the speakers in your home that is providing an intimate ambiance, nicely coupled with the candles and romantically prepared food? Sound. What's that coming off of that concert stage that has you throwing yourself about in a spasmodic heave and ho? Sound. Early churches and monasteries were built to provide the most effective acoustic delivery possible in order that the song being sung in them would enhance the spiritual experience.

We are sound beings, no if, ands, or maybes. You should use sound as a tool to display your appreciation. Leave no room for the imagination. Have your customers exiting your doors knowing without a shadow of a doubt how thankful you are for them.

3. Lastly but certainly not least, deliver the product as competently and exactly as promised. Which brings me to my next point:

Your product also presents a grand opportunity. Does your product work? Are you good at what you do? It doesn't matter how affable your Customer Server is, how comfortable he/she makes the customer feel. If what the customer is purchasing is not what they want or isn't what they expected, the CX failed. Imagine sitting in a taxi cab with the best taxi cab driver you've ever met. The driver is so funny. The only difference between that cab and a comedy club is motion. There's a big problem, however. You both are really lost and the driver has no clue how to "unloose" you. For me, being lost would make this scenario the worst taxi experience ever, despite how wonderfully the driver and I got along. The purpose for hailing a taxi wasn't to find a new BFF. You wanted to get from point A to point B. Well, the sole reason for the cab was not accomplished; the product was not delivered properly; it was a CX Failure.

So, it could easily be said, Cx is or is found in your product or service. Encapsulated inside your business, on a molecular level, your CX is inextricably part of what you do. I know technically you sell men suits; but, in every suit Cx is represented. Customer satisfaction is found in whether or not the customer likes your suits. Customer experience is affected by the suit itself, totally apart from the personality of the sales person.

Quality is a synonym for Customer Service. This is why liquor commercials stress the pain-staking aging process of their spirits, why wineries are constantly swirling their wondrous aperitif in expensive crystal decanters, and why southern restaurants proudly recant their slow-roasting process that causes the meat to fall off of the bone. It all paints a picture of "involved effort." Effort translates in to an exhaustive expenditure of time and time equates altruistic affection. So, the purveyor's delivery of a product is actually a heart-felt utterance of love. Your time, affection, and concern for your customer should be blaringly apparent in your product.

Pastor Rick Warren, the author of the world-renowned book "The Purpose Driven Life," once said: "The best use of life is love. **_The best expression of love is time_**. The best time to love is now." Scientists have written extensively about the effect of time: *time* with your children can make them more confident; too much *time* at work can have a negative effect on your health; less *time* in isolation and social participation could affect your mental health positively. Time isn't just the chronological distance between today and tomorrow. It's weightier than that. Time represents breath lost. It represents irretrievable seconds and hours. A thousand dollars is worth significantly more today than it did two decades ago. Ask a parent about time while they are watching their "baby" drive off to college. Ask someone about time after a visit to their mailbox, there to find a crispy AARP card in mint condition. Time involves more than an alarm clock.

These qualities of time should be ostensibly intertwined in your product. There's no substitute for a high-grade product. Quality products are conversations between the product owner and the customer. "Here's my time (which we've learned weighs a lot) Here's my sweat and tears." "I'm willing to part with it only as a token of my affection to you, at a price that is equal to my precious expenditure." If you have a janitorial service, this conversation is found in every broom or mop stroke. Why would you give away, or sell for that matter, something that means a lot to you to someone that isn't worthy of your item. Bottom line is, your product quality articulates your affection for yourself and your customer. The time expended to develop a product is a direct correlation to your thoughts and affection to yourself or/and your customer.

Make the unspoken words to your customers be one of positivity. Show your kind regard for them by selling a product of significant worth, worth to you and them. Again, quality is a synonym for Cx.

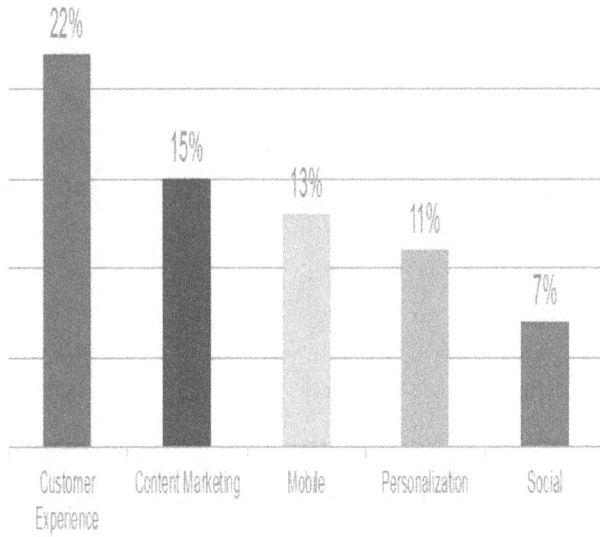

Study By Digital Marketing Trends, asking consumers what they prefer…

CX Versus Personalization

Personalization is seen as an attempt from the product owner or industry professionals to improve customer experience by creating methods that make purchasing faster and easier. Experts have studied their customers and become intimately familiar with their purchasing habits. They have identified patterns and created amenities, aids, and offers that supposedly make the patron's life easier. They make checking-in to a hotel quicker, grocery check-outs faster, bank transaction quicker.

"Cost Of Poor Customer," published by Genesys Global Survey, I learned that 78% of consumers prefer competent customer interaction as opposed to product personalization, meaning "treat me nicely" is better than "make me comfortable." As a business owner or manager, that sentence should have you kicking your heels and performing the most elaborate jig that your body can muster. Here you are going above and beyond to buy décor to make your book store look like Downton Abbey, picking up highway debris, nailing it to the wall of your yogurt shop to accomplish an ambiance that you think will cater to your preferred clientele. Now you realize that you should have spent an equal if not most of that time interviewing the candidates that will stand behind your counter serving your customers.

This would explain the uncanny penchant I had to drive 5 miles out of my way to fill up at Mr. Patel's station. Let me tell you, Mr. Patel's gas station was far from personalized. I'll give you the best picture that I can conjure to illustrate Mr. Patel's store and its relation to being personalized. Imagine yourself drowning in the middle of the ocean. The only thing that can save you from a watery demise is Mr. Patel and his store's personalization. Now, imagine yourself dead, bloated, floating on top of the ocean like a buoy. Get the picture? This guy sat behind a 4 inch, fiber glass reinforced plastic encasement – ala The Pope Mobile. Mr. Patel's restroom floors were so sticky that it sounded like you were opening a wallet from the 80's when you walked. I swear, though, when I walked in to his store, the reaction on his face every time he saw me would lead you to believe that I was his long lost relative or at the very least a profoundly intimate acquaintance. Mr. Patel didn't know my name; but, he walked the extra mile to make me feel comfortable. He was kind enough to "throw me a bone" and feign a laugh in response to every joke I would tell. "Mr. Patel, it's as hot as Hades outside," I would say. Mr. Patel would drop a roll of pennies writhing in an uncontrollable guffaw. My thoughts: "Now, Mr. Patel you know damn well it's not that funny." Part of me, however, appreciated his attempt to make my experience a positive one.

I was far from the only person that decided to disregard the dubious space-age adhesion Mr. Patel had applied to his floors. He served hundreds of customers a day. The community in which he lived had awarded him with numerous awards that he mounted decorously about his store. You wouldn't be able to see the awards, however. Mr. Patel purposely superimposed those awards with photos of his customers, photos of his customer's children, photos of the local little league football, basketball, and soccer teams, clearly sending a message as to what was most important to him.

He had plenty of competition too, a store directly across from him, two additional stores a few blocks away, a veritable petroleum oasis one exit south of him. If these stores were Christmas gifts, Mr. Patel's competition would be the newest gaming system, stocked with all the most current and hottest new games. Mr. Patel's store would be a sticky slinky. People drove up to Mr. Patel's store to see him and "Oh, yeah! Let me get some gas while I'm here." In 7 years, most of his competition eventually boarded up their windows, and locked their doors, even the gigantic multi-product, gas and restaurant stores were no match for Mr. Patel. The public made their choice. They chose being treated nicely over slurpies and sausage biscuits. They chose the warmth of community over personalization. Have I mentioned that Mr. Patel's store was far from personalized? His CX made everyone feel comfortable. And, everyone rewarded him with their business.

Don't get me wrong, I'm all for making things easier. I'm drastically a happier person the more "Sesame Street" things are for me. When I go to my cell phone dealer on a busy weekend and there's a greeter there to input my name in to his computer generated, electronic waiting list amongst the intense fray of other cell phone enthusiasts, which in turn allows me to peruse the store and not have to physically stand in line, this makes me happy. However, given the choice, I would just as easily suffer waiting in a serpentine line that stretched in to the next county as opposed to having all the inanimate creature comforts that makes waiting easier and a clueless, butt-hole cellphone representative.

Harbinger Kang, the Senior Director of Corporate Affairs for Cisco, conducted an experiment that focused on human behavior, collaboration, and their effect on productivity and interwork related relationships. They tested many creature comforts that were supposed to make Cisco employees lives much easier like video conferencing, desktop sharing, and instant messaging. Their study definitively demonstrated that productivity and collaboration was inextricably dependent upon human interaction. According to Kang one of his employees stated: "We need to get back to intimacy."

One of the most disgustingly offensive contraptions in the world of customer service is that module that some restaurants place on the table so that the customers can pay for their meal without waiting on the waiter or waitress. Nothing says more "I'm too busy to interact" than that ridiculous machine. The restaurant is missing out on a prime opportunity to get feedback, to apologize for any mistake known or unknown, to seal the deal on their hopeful, upcoming return. Retrieving the check and issuing change is a perfect time for reconnaissance and fact gathering which is holistically lost by personalization.

Don't let making the lives of your customers more comfortable morph in to distant behavior and shunning of them. Ultimately, there is no substitute to one-on-one communication and relationships. Mr. Kang's experiment proved that personal interaction bolstered a feeling of community and discontinued territorial behavior in collective assignments and projects. Don't overly computerize your business. Leave some room for Cx that is provided by face-to-face communication, Cx that allows the humanistic characteristic of your business to be experienced. This what your customers want and need more than self-serving grocery isle or the option to visit your website to search for the answer they would much rather obtain from you directly.

Here's another stat that should have you twerking in excitement. In a recent study conducted by American Express, they found that "73% of customers are willing to pay more for good service." How much more, you say? How's 12% more if the product is accompanied by excellent customer service," according to Amex. I've often wondered how much of an implosion would occur in the universe if a business owner or product owner made CX the focal point of the business not the product. We've just learned that the product itself plays second chair to service. What would happen if the product was an afterthought? Those loud car dealer commercials would go something like this: "C'mon down to Rob's Automotive! Where the comfortable, no pressure environment, the warm, pleasant non-beguiling sales people will cater to you every need! You need some time to think before jumping in to a major purchase? No problem! You don't want the deluxe model but the less expensive, reasonably priced vehicle? No problem! Come to see our sales professionals; but, leave with a car."

Genuine, memorable CX covers a lot of sin. You may not have the most aesthetically pleasing building in your market. You may not have all the latest creature comforts. Your competition may be more "LOL" and "Emoji" savvy than you. Combat that deficiency with the best CX you are physically able to find. It's what 73% of your customers want instead of the items your rivals have.

Often, especially in the out-set, we fall in to the trap of concentrating on the non-essential aspects of our business. Shop owners are overly concerned about matching uniforms. Sales professional set their eyes on the best business cards, when really, according to studies, our customers would equally enjoy your winning personality and your competency and a sticky note with your name, cell number, and an email address. You have a restaurant with mixed-matched wobbly chairs? 3 out of 4 of your customer would ignore that issue if your waitress has an awesome personality. You have a carpet cleaning company and you drive around town in your wife's mini-van, with no logo along with your carpet extraction equipment? 3 out of 4 of your customers would disregard your transportation and less professional appearance if your competency distracts them. Your customers want and are eagerly willing to pay more for great Cx over personalization.

Pre-Cx Rules

In a former life, I worked in the hospitality industry as what is called a Task Force General Manager. Cool title isn't it? It always made me think of the movie "Men In Black" or "X-Files." I was assigned to limited service hotels across the country for brief amounts of time, many of which were owned by major brand names like Hilton, IHG, Choice, Wyndham to name a few. Each of these brands required the hotel to achieve and maintain a particular level of customer satisfaction and problem resolution. These hotels were graded on a weekly, monthly, and annual basis based upon the surveys submitted by the guests. If the properties failed to reach the required level of guest satisfaction or if a certain percentage of surveys were returned with negative feedback or comments the hotels suffered. In turn, the owners of those hotels would suffer by way of fines and fees and letters and emails that would tacitly say: "Get your act together, damn it!" Consequentially, the owners would discuss amongst themselves ways to torture the General Managers (GM). Thus the GM would scour his brain to find subtle but painful ways to share that experience with his staff. And round and round she goes! Where she stops nobody knows! Many of the brands would request/ demand of the ownership to remove their brand name if the hotel wasn't able to maintain respectable customer service scores. I've experienced monetarily profitable hotels threatened by their brand to fix their CX or take down their signs. Can you imagine that? Enormous international brands like Hilton and Marriott who obtain sometimes 15 – 30 percent of total revenue in franchise fees monthly, disregarding and denying their financial stipends because a particular hotel is damaging their brand name with unsatisfactory customer service? Customer Service is a big deal.

I've been assigned hotels where it would be easier to find cohesion in Congress than to find a positive comment about the property. From my experience I've learned 3 things:

1. I have the patience of Job on Xanax

2. Despite the hotel, the location, the employees, or the clientele excellent customer service (CX) is nevertheless obtainable. With proper training and extensive knowledge of the product and themselves, the CX phoenix can rise from the ashes of improper customer relations.

3. Finally, I learned not to underestimate the importance of well-trained, well placed CX.

One more statistic: Ruby Newell-Legner wrote a book called "Understanding Customers." In it she wrote: "96% of consumers do not report their negative experience. Of that 96%, 91% will not return as a result. I'm sure there's no dancing after reading that one. It is nevertheless one of the most important stats you should be aware as a business owner.

I think we are all aware of the fact that we are just seconds away from being enveloped by a financial collapse. I think the Big Depression of 2008 taught is that. What we neglect to fully understand is that our financial destruction does not only lie in the hands of banks and Wall Street. It rests in the hands of our customers and the destructive power of the word of mouth.

Research as early as 1944 has shown that word of mouth (WOM) is fundamentally more effective than any print or video advertisement. The reasoning behind the effectiveness harkens back to our last topic: "Interpersonal Relationships." The customer possesses in remarkable abundance all of the components of the power of persuasion. In the Republic, Aristotle taught us that logos, pathos, and ethos are the driving force behind any speaker and their conversation or speech. Let's deal with each one, showing how each disgruntled customer wields each and how they affect any potential customer.

Ethos: Your unhappy customer holds with a white-knuckle grip the onus of ethics. They believe firmly that it is their responsibility to inform others of their experience and your ineptness. It doesn't matter if the desire to school the world of your mistakes is a gesture of humanitarianism or simply a bent toward revenge or to fundamentally destroy you and your ability to feed your family. This new-found mission carries with it mesmerizing persuasion. Many-a war have been won by warriors guided by a sense of ethics. An equal amount of laws have been revised in this country by ethic-fueled protests and civil disobedience. People involved in actions that are believed to be ethically correct can move mountains. It will be with this passion your malcontented patrons will inform other potential customers. And they, like a crescendo of falling dice, will cause other customers to have the same disaffection for you.

Ethics not only has the strength of a powerful fuel to accomplish a momentous task, but it affords authenticity that is easily interpreted by others. The words of a person speaking with conviction from an ethical and/or personal vantage point often go uninvestigated and become perceived truth. The interpersonal relationship between the speaker and the listener plays a big role in the ultimate acceptance of the message. The passion off the delivery, notwithstanding, is equally effective in the whole-sale compliance of the communique.

Go to any political rally and you will realize this unfortunate truth: the ratio of disinformation to emotion is all but guaranteed to be one to one. The audience being doused with less than factual information is hypnotized by histrionic and thus lulled in to welcoming the words spoken from a podium as certitude. The speaker tosses substantiality to the wind and utilizes heart-felt (ethics) expressions to deliver the point. How many times have politicians promised something? We, in the moment, enter in to the full throws of elation and jubilee shout the name of our beloved candidate; later, to use their names as an epithet. The statesman's ethic-fuel words were automatically received as truth. It is inextricably part of politics and it could be an integral part of the demise of your business. A potential customer will accept the words of a passionate acquaintance swiftly. So begins the invalidation of your reputation and, if not resolved quickly, your business.

Logos: An unhappy customer uses logic to get their message across. It just makes sense not to patronize your business considering the absolute catastrophe that occurred. How smart is it for someone to use your website after an experienced user details the difficulty of navigating it? We've all seen it before, the ardent recapping of a friend's terrible ordeal, how they repaint in vivid detail their disappointing experience, revisiting every moment in fiery detail. One would have to be an imbecilic masochist to utilize your service after the friend is finished. It becomes an indication of one's intelligence not to use you. Don't make it smart to avoid you.

Pathos: Passion. We've discussed this briefly, earlier in the Ethos section. Personal involvement equates identity, who and what we have consciously assigned ourselves as an accurate representation. The activities to which we are intimately committed could easily be icons of our being. Because we are pinioned on a cellular level with these activities, we defend them furiously, protecting them in the same manner as if we were being bodily attacked. Your unhappy customer reacts to your Cx failure as an attack on them. As stated before, it will be with this white-heated pathos they will approach all those with a listening ear. Keep in mind, now, these are the customer that did not bother to inform you of their disappointment. These are the silent but dangerous disgruntled customers.

Listen, you're not conscious of it, but the grim reaper is stalking you, stealthily matching your every move. Your waitress accidentally poured sweat tea on a customer and didn't apologize to the fullest extent? You can bank on that customer revisiting that instance numerously throughout their existence on this planet. And predicated upon how often your team drops the ball (or drops the picture of sweet tea) will determine the size of the army of disgruntled customers chanting like the Israelites in the Battle of Jericho to make the walls of your business come crumbling down. The unseen ones make up 50% of your unhappy clients. So, like a pipe leaking CO_2, unseen, no smell, no prior warning your customers are slowly choosing someone else. You close your store one day after a long day of selling, and you return the next day to find your business diminished significantly, and you have no clue why. You didn't see it coming. Your CX killed your business. The people you have representing you, representing your product, the people you have in front of your customers have sucked the life-blood out of your dreams.

Jeff Staton/ Nice Is Not Enough!

Study By Bureau Of Labor Statistics displaying the benefits of having an education

Unemployment rates and earnings by educational attainment, 2016

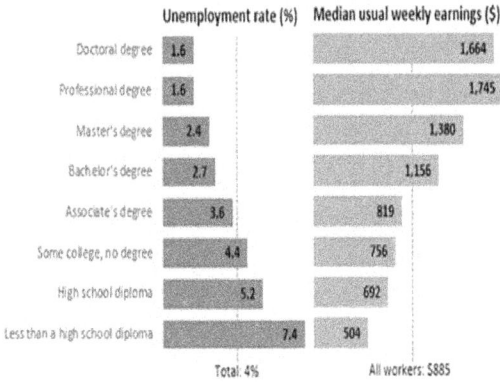

Educational attainment	Unemployment rate (%)	Median usual weekly earnings ($)
Doctoral degree	1.6	1,664
Professional degree	1.6	1,745
Master's degree	2.4	1,380
Bachelor's degree	2.7	1,156
Associate's degree	3.6	819
Some college, no degree	4.4	756
High school diploma	5.2	692
Less than a high school diploma	7.4	504
	Total: 4%	All workers: $885

Note: Data are for persons age 25 and over. Earnings are for full-time wage and salary workers.
Source: U.S. Bureau of Labor Statistics, Current Population Survey.

Before You Place Educate:

If nothing else, I want you to understand just how intricate Cx is. There's so much to consider. It is my opinion that genuine, memorable CX begins first with hiring right people, then training the right people. By right people I mean bringing aboard quality, suitable, willing, and capable people to represent you and your product or service. Once that illusive, almost fairytale-like person is found there are a few things he/she should know prior to being placed in front of your customers.

One of the strangest things I've ever encountered (besides the woman who actually said yes to marry me) was a vegetarian waitress of a steakhouse. I know that sounds like a punch line, but it really happened. Had I not known my favorite cut, had I possessed a wild hair that evening and asked the waitress for her suggestion, what do you think would have been her answer? She could answer NOTHING, nothing honestly and nothing genuinely. She could have fired off some canned, precooked, half-baked answer, something she had been told. I wasn't asking her friends, her co-workers. I was asking her.

There are at least 3 assumptions we are able to make from this Vegan Steakhouse Waitress scenario:

1. That waitress was not really hired to sell. I'm sure the hiring supervisor or HR department had prerequisites and pertinent criteria that they used as the bases of their hiring preference. It is fair to say that selling or the competency for selling did not exist amongst them. I find a considerable amount of confidence in making that statement because you can only sell things with which you are familiar first hand. You would never purchase anything of importance from someone that would say to you: "Well, I heard that it was a good idea." Maybe that's an assumption I shouldn't make about you. Maybe you are an adventurous (by adventurous I mean really dumb) person that finds pleasure in rolling the dice when it comes to purchasing. Personally, I find the diploma on the pharmacy wall indicating the pharmacist studied a lot before she decided on a career suggesting medication. It eases my insecurities seeing those weird letters after my psychologist name, allowing me comfort in knowing that I'm spilling my guts to a learned individual and not someone as jacked up as me. (And yes, jacked-up is technical term.) This Vegan Steakhouse Waitress was hired simply to take orders, to relay a script to the cook, and on to the next customer. Listen, minor facilitation is not

serving the customer. Any real server will tell you that just repeating to the cook what the customer said, fetching what the customer requested, and obtaining payment doesn't touch the tip of the ice burg as it relates to being a real server.

2. You know what else? It is as plain as the nose on our faces that manager of that restaurant really wasn't too fond of selling either. It's clear also that he or she were about as concerned about their customers as a fish in the ocean is concerned about rain. Obviously the manager's main concern was having someone available to take orders. The periphery duties that are attached to being a waitress such as being able to make suggestions to better the customer's experiences were low on his totem pole of priorities.

3. There are assumptions we can make about the owner of the restaurant based upon the decisions of the manager too. Why are you hiring people that have not experienced your product first-hand? Doctors spend years studying and training before they come close to picking up a scalpel. Teachers spend numerous hours preparing nightly before they start class. Why? (1) They hold the goals they are trying to accomplish in high regard. They understand that their students

and patients and the treatment of them have a direct link to the success they are attempting to accomplish. (2) They hold the student and patient in high regard. They care about them. When you place people in front of your customers that are unprepared, lacking full knowledge of what they represent, you are displaying the level of your affection for your customers and your product and service. In subsequent chapters we will discuss what effect confidence, knowledge, and being genuine will have on your Customer Sever and your customers. It is knowledge that will make your CX shine like a beacon in a raging storm. It's the sense of genuineness that will cause every customer that walks in to your store to buy ferociously. You are causing tremendous damage to your business and brand by putting uneducated, inexperienced – as it relates to your product- people in front of your customers.

We discussed previously the detrimental effects of WOM and what are the active ingredients of WOM that will cause you to lose customers. Well, conversely those active ingredients are in effect in the WOM of a fully educated Customer Server. They will possess the Pathos or passion from personal experience, the Ethos or ethics because they, now, believe in your product, and the logos or logic from having intellectual engagement with the product. Part of the training process should be educating the new hire through experience. No team member should be allowed to represent you if they have not tried your product. Notice the eyes of a team member, selling something they've experienced first-hand and liked it. Educating prior to placing should be a rule of thumb for you

False words are not only evil in themselves, but they infect the soul with evil.

Plato, Phaedo

Sell, Don't Manipulate:

Have you ever encountered that person, either at a car dealership or an electronic store, and although the words they spoke were seemingly 100% friendly and unthreatening, you still felt like they were hiding something? Your ears heard all the nice words, but your heart heard the hissing noises of venomous snakes. You just knew they were going try to up sell the hell out of you. So, instead of focusing on the product you came to purchase you spent your time practicing in your mind how you would fire off the "No thank you's" or the "Not right now's."

Our customers deal with a lot of potential purchasing hazards: identity thieves, personal finance problems, internet scams. With these in mind, our customers have erected a protective emotional wall between the customer service professional and themselves. They walk in to your store like a western gun fighter, brandishing the shiny memories from past encounters. These memories are resting in an easily accessible part of the brain like a holster and six-shooter at the fingertip of a cowboy, quick to be whipped out. Their goal is to never experience those memories again. You as a Customer Server represent the embodiment of those memories. Sadly too often you receive the misplaced emotions and treatment as a result of those memories. Nevertheless you must weather through those misguided emotions; you have to chisel through the emotional bastion. To achieve the best customer service and/or customer experience, the Customer Server must be able to lower that wall. There are many ways to achieve this but the best ways is being real.

In all honesty, prudent business practices dictate that we up sell. Truth be told, we are in business to make money. On the other hand, however, savvy business people have conjured up ways to force a sale, whether a consumer wants it or not. They've created ways to get the customer to pay more for items or services, knowing that there are other items equally effective and far less expensive. They verbally lure the consumer to purchase additional or ancillary items along with the primary purchase. One of my favorite people to dislike (after barbers with bad breath) is car sales people. After you have financially pinioned yourself to these people for the next 4 years, they have the audacity to push mud flaps. Really, dude? I just spent 45k of my hard earned money; and, that demon of avarice in your head couldn't let me out of the door without getting you to squeeze me for an additional $150? It makes me feel uncomfortable. What about when you take your car in for service? I had one mechanic   attempt to sell me 4 new tires when I knew the ones currently on the car were perfectly fine. Another tried to sell me space-age window cleaner, supposedly able to magically thwart rain and mud. It had an amazing ability to shield the car from those stray rocks flying from off those trucks. Those guys are relentless.

Every time I think of manipulative salespeople (or manipulative people in general) an image of witches and warlocks surfaces in my mind. (SN: Strangely enough on the other hand, when I think of witches and warlocks, images of politicians surfaces in my mind. Weird, huh?) Truthfully, what is the essence of witchcraft? It is the efforts of someone to get you to do something you wouldn't do normally if you were not under some spell. That is exactly what forceful, lying, finessing salespeople are doing, trying to get the customer to purchase something they wouldn't without the guile. They are witches and warlocks, making all attempts to lure you in to their layer, to boil you in their soup, to make you their minion, to suck the blood out of you. Ok, maybe not that dramatic but very close in my opinion. They want your money and they will say anything, create any façade to entice you to lose your grip on your wallet.

Again, I fully understand the idea behind up selling. I'm an hotelier remember? Up selling is in my DNA. There's a "U" chromosome in all GM's. I cannot guess the number of times I sold a suite when I had plenty of less expensive rooms available. What separates me from witches and warlocks is my willingness to down sell, to accommodate the customer, my willingness to – now get this; it's phenomenal- *let the customer get what they want and that's it.* I didn't fall in to some apparent deep depression in front of the customer. I didn't suggest that my family will go without winter wood for the fire because the guest did not rent the room I preferred. Sure, I'll certainly mention the more expensive item; but, if the customer clearly indicates he/she wants the lesser expensive item then I will sell that product as I would the deluxe item.

A business that can justify manipulation in their selling efforts and business practices are making statements about their product. A good product does not need to be forcefully or surreptitiously pushed upon any one. By using coercive tactics to sell your product you are saying that your product can't stand on its own merits. You are saying: "I have this weak product and the only way to sell it, I will have to lie, cheat, create a mirage to get people to pay attention." That's sad. Why would you want to sell someone a product that isn't up to par? Haven't we evolved beyond selling snake oil?

Here are four signs that someone is attempting to manipulate you:

1. **Lying:** If it sounds too good to be true, it probably is. Withholding or altering information is a manipulator's first choice in their coercive tactics. If it's a significant purchase, house, car, large capital expenditures, I would do my homework before venturing out on a mission to buy. At least know the basics before you speak to someone.

2. **Repetition:** After you have clearly established what you want, what you are expecting, what you are willing to buy or pay, if the merchant continues to push something you don't want. They are attempting to manipulate you. Be concise, clear, to the point. Say exactly what you mean. Don't generalize, using words like: maybe, possibly, or could.

3. **Talkative:** If you are with a merchant that will seldom allow you to speak, they are constantly interrupting and cutting you off in midsentence, spewing incredibly long sentences and paragraphs. You are being manipulated. A company that doesn't want to hear what you have to say doesn't want your business.

4. **Mood Changes:** The sweet, kind, hilariously funny sales person suddenly becomes a demon possessed drill sergeant when you mention that you are not interested is another sign of manipulation. They in turn try to make you feel guilty. "So, you are not interested in making money?" "So, you're not interested in protecting your family?" These are telltale signs of manipulation. Hang up. Walkout the door. End the conversation.

If you encounter any of these 4 behaviors, even if you really want the product, please be aware that for some reason that company feels the need to coerce you. Coercion is not a good sign that you are about to purchase a good product or venture in to a good investment. I like the CarMax approach. This is the price, no haggling. Take it or leave it. That is a sign of confidence.

I managed a hotel in the mid-west. This hotel was profitable one. It wasn't, however, accomplishing its full potential as it related to revenue. The most significant challenge I had in getting the hotel to its full potential was the Sales Coordinator. Bless her heart. She was a person with the perfect personality, ebullient, fun, and giddy. The guests loved her. Every client she met would write raving reviews about her. She would attend local city events and dazzle everyone in the room. She was 10 times more popular than I was as the GM. If her job was to be Ms. Personality and make everyone like her, she would be an industry guru. That was not her job, unfortunately. She was hired to sell sleeping rooms and meeting space. She accomplished this mission by offering profound discounts. She would never quote the actual price of the rooms or of the meeting room. She would discount right off the bat. When clients called to book groups (10 rooms or more) she would throw the meeting space in for free if they chose our hotel over our competitors. If that wouldn't work, she would discount the rooms even further. I could have sworn I heard her tell a client she would *pay them* if they stayed with us. (No, not really; but you get the point.) She had a love affair with discounting. She strongly believed that the guests expected discounts; and it was the discounts that would sway them from our competitors. She manipulated with discounts and freebees.

After learning that our property had only accomplished an unfortunate $10 spread under our lower-end competitors, I had a "come to Jesus" meeting with my Sales person that was dispensing discounts like a water sprinkler. I told her that she lacked confidence in her product. I asked her what was necessary for her to obtain the confidence in the product she was selling. Her discounting reflex was a sign that she was not confident, that she did not believe in what she was selling on a personal level. I asked her how much did she believe the sleeping rooms and meeting space was worth. She gave me a number. I said to sell them at that price and don't go any lower.

Manipulation is the physical manifestation of unbelief. If the vendor believed in the product there would be no need for manipulation. If you believe in yourself and your business, toss manipulation to the wind. You don't need it. You have a viable product. You offer something that is needed; it answers a question; and, it supplies a need. When I started my business, initially I felt the need to have a script when I was telemarketing. I felt that I had to use particular words to fool the person answering the phone in order to speak to the person that would hire me. I stopped that. I simply expressed my intentions exactly and informed them exactly who I was. I didn't feel the need to be guileful. I was confident. I am a value-added potential partner. Speak to me for your betterment or not to your determent. Be confident. Get away from being sneaky and shady. You are worth more than that.

Have you ever regretted any purchase? Have you ever fallen victim to a salesperson's manipulation and purchased something you really didn't want or need? Remember the last time you fell for the illusion that the sales sirens were portraying? Their sales pitch lulled you to sleep. When you woke up at home you realized that you purchased a ship wreck. After realizing that you are now the owner of something far less than what you paid, how did you feel? What is it called that you were experiencing at that moment? It's called **regret**, right? You are now wishing you had the ability to kick yourself in the buttocks. Thank God you caught the flu and missed a week of Yoga class. In the light of the regret you are now nurturing, how would you rate the actual overall experience of your purchase? The regret you have throws a dark cloud over everything that happened at the store and prior to getting home. Everything at the store may have gone perfectly. So well, now, you and the sales person are dating and seriously talking about adding each other on Facechat or something. That all changed when your newfangled doohickey didn't work. The malfunctioning product destroyed the experience in its entirety.

CX doesn't end when your customers leave, or when they hang up or log off. We learned already that CX is an inextricable part of the molecules of your product. The products itself paints the CX picture for our customers. The customer has a wonderful time at your store. They get home and the product works wonderfully. We'll call that the Norman Rockwell experience. On the other hand, however, the customer has a wonderful time at your store, gets home and product is defective: your CX paints a medieval Black Death portrait or regret. As a result your business is stained. Your reputation is scarred. Sure, your manipulation worked. You got the money. The customer took the product. What is going to happen in return is a regret-fueled word-of-mouth campaign that will harm you irrevocably. The saying years ago was that for every one disgruntled customer, 10 potential customers are informed of the incident. Nowadays, it has increased 10 fold with social media. It is possible today that for every 1, 10 million are informed.

You want a viable business? You want to be seen as business person of integrity? Manipulation will not help you in that venture. It ultimately causes customer regret. And regret can morph in to a really big nail in the coffin of your business and its success.

What you probably don't know is our customers – all of them, even you and I- suffer from Posttraumatic Purchasing Syndrome (PTPS). PTPS is the result of years of beguiling up selling: buying the laptop _and_ the 20 year maintenance agreement that you pay monthly, which in turn caused you to pay for your laptop 13 times over, or buying a subscription to the website _and_ the all-to-necessary magazine subscription. It was the years of forceful and unwanted solicitation, years of purchasing faulty products that has caused you now to walk in fear concerning purchasing. You have erected a dense emotional bastion that protects you from witches and warlocks. Our customers have too. They throw up the emotional bastion immediately before calling your call center, before logging on to your website. You don't believe me? Ok, when was the last time you jumped for joy when you saw a clothing store sales person? You and I both know that clothing sales people make your teeth itch. When that sales persons walks up to you, do you welcome her warmly with open arms? Or, do you do what most of us do: reach for the 6 inch, stainless steel switchblade that grandpa used in the Civil War and say: "I'm just looking." When you are car shopping, does the sight of the car salesperson walking toward you cause the music of Kenny G play in your head? Or do you react like most people, pray for an earth quake so that the car person will fall in a hole before they reach you?

The way we cringe, and get angry when a Customer Server attempts to help us is a sign of

PTPS.   Past hurts, disappointments, negative experiences have created a bad taste in your mouth for sales people.   The only thing that makes customers feel comfortable about lowering the emotional wall is GENUINE CX.

There are many components to make up Genuine CX.   One is integrity.   If customers sense you are honest, if they don't sense that they are prey but valued patrons, they will gladly remove any protective barrier and allow you to serve them to the fullest extent.   Manipulation, forceful tactics will not accomplish that goal in any way.   Remember this formula:

Comfort + Positive Experience + Excellent Product
= Return or New Customer.

Manipulation always = regret and negative outlook
on your business or product.

By appreciation, we make excellence in others our own property. -Voltaire

Keep CX Zones Sterile:

I'm a huge Redskins fan, for good or worse. I have been since I was a teenager. A few years back I was given a Skins jersey. I was ecstatic! I hugged it. I caressed it. I took pictures of it. Since, I've probably worn it a total of 10 times. It is certainly a prize possession. When I wear it I begin to strut. My gait becomes bouncy. My arms swing at a wider angle. A noticeable expression of happiness rests upon my face. This jersey is certainly a prize possession. My daughter is the biggest Daddy's Girl you can imagine. At age 12 she climbed on me like I was jungle gym. She's a habitual hugger too. She used to grab me at any moment and hug me. Any other day I would revel warmly suffused in her demonstration of affection. On the day I wear my jersey, she knows to approach with caution. I've used words like "headlock," "disownment," and "sin and eternal hellfire" to get that point across. Did I say my jersey is a prize possession yet?

If you are around me when I pull out my jersey, there would be no questions in your mind about my feelings for it. It is demonstrated by my actions. Your affection for your customers is demonstrated by your actions also. A good way to show how much worth you have invested in your customers is by keeping your CX Zones sterile.

First, what are CX Zones? CX Zones are any place where your customers' experience can be affected, any place where a sale can be affected, any place where a customer can hear or see you is considered a CX Zone. This means, then, your CX Zones stretches beyond the four walls of your store. This means your parking lot has the potential to be a CX Zone. Your restroom has the potential to be a CX Zone. (SN: Although restrooms can be CX Zones, use your own discretion whether or not to actually server customers there.) If a sale can be affected negatively or positively by any of your actions, you are in a CX Zone. And these zones must be kept sterile.

What do I mean by sterile and how do I keep them so? Imagine an operating room. Doctors and nurses go to great lengths to prepare for every operation: there are pre-op meetings, there's final examination of the patients charts and x-rays to ensure everyone is on the same page. Then there is a massive sterilization process: sterile gloves, sterile masks; sterile operating utensils, sterile hands – all done prior to the operation. Finally, the operating door is closed. Lights are turned on. The process is underway. No one is allowed in the room at this point. And if someone must enter, they must go through the sterilization process that everyone did prior to the operation.

What does all the meetings, prepping, the sterilization, the protective measures tell you? It should tell you that something is going on in that operating room that is very important and sensitive.

It should tell you that all the participants are going to great lengths to handle whatever is going on with a considerable amount of care. There's something quite important in that operating room and on that operating table.

Your store, your website, your service is the operating room. Your customers are the important patient inside. You must go to great lengths to maintain and protect that environment against contamination that would thwart a sale and a positive experience for your customers. Here's an example. Sally caught her boyfriend cheating at the Motel 5 ½. It is reasonable to understand and expect poor Sally to be unhappy about this revelation. One can easily imagine Sally's disposition being distraught, at the very least disappointed, right? The next morning Sally goes to work at the CX Center where she answers the phones. Sally is so sad that her voice illustrates it in every word. Here posture at work leaves no room for the imagination. Sally is not happy. Here are a couple of questions:

1. *Can Sally's voice affect a sale?*

2. *Can Sally's disposition and appearance cause a negative experience for the customer?*

If the answer is yes, then Sally is contaminating the CX Zone and should be quickly removed.

You must require ALL team members to leave all personal issues and hardship that contaminate your sterile environment at home, or at least require them to be able to mask the trouble they are experiencing while in the CX Zone. Please understand enforcing Sterile CX Zones is not being insensitive. By all means be compassionate and understanding. Don't bark at them and demand that they squelch their feelings and be positive. Nevertheless, protective measures must be taken immediately. In an operating room a person's life is at stake. One wrong move and a life could end. Believe me, explaining to the newly departed's family member that the doctor's wife or husband is cheating on them, and he/she just wasn't themselves in the operating room will most probably be less than acceptable. When we hold our CX to the same level a doctor holds the patient, very few excuses would be acceptable by you.

You got to keep your CX Zones sterile, no negativity, nothing that will cause you to lose a patient. CX is a big deal and as an owner, department head, or supervisor you must make sure your Customer Servers are able to represent you prior to placing them in front of your customers. They must:

1. Be fully knowledgeable of your company and your product before they are allowed to work for you.

2. Must understand that you run a business of integrity. Forcing, manipulating, and

coercing the customers to purchase items they don't want or need will not be tolerated.

3. Understands that while they are in the CX Zone, like an actor when the red light is on, they are on! They are expected to perform and make all customers experiences wonderful.

Chapter 2

company centric	customer centric
revenue	value
short term	long term
relationship	engagement
message	content
managed expectations	known expectations
proprietary solution	ecosystem
interaction	experience

According To Esteban Kolsky, CEO of ThinkJar, a customer strategy consultant, the above chart describes the differences between Company Centric and Customer Centric businesses.

Your CX Represents You

What is branding? When I think about branding visions of my childhood appear in my mind. Most Sunday evenings, I sat on the couch after church watching black and white westerns with my parents.   I   never   understood   why   those cowpokes would place a branding iron on those poor cows. Until one cow-thieving individual stole one of the Riffle Man's cows. The Riffle Man confronted the thief and proved that the cow was his by unveiling his brand he had hidden in a special place on the cow. I was like: "Whoa, you can't deny that! You low-down, lily-livered polecat."   That scar burned in to the skin of that cow was irrefutable proof that it belong to the Riffle Man.

The brand was something the Riffle Man had created and was totally dissimilar to any cattle brand anywhere. That brand represented his farm, his home, his life. It was The Riffle Man's fingerprint.

It's all about being distinct. We will go in to detail about originality later. Before you can be original you have to know who you are. What image are you trying to display? Who, as a business person, do you want other business people and your patrons to see? Are you a family person and want that aspect of your life to be apparent through your product, through your business? Are you socially conscience person and you want that aspect to be apparent? These are pertinent questions you have to pose to yourself (1) before you start a business and (2) before you hire Customer Servers you want representing you and the image you are trying to portray.

Continuity is profoundly consequential. There must be a smooth flow, from your vision to your implementation of the vision, to the people facilitating the vision. It can't be choppy. The state of being of your business will illustrate its apparent quality or character. Believe it or not our customers can sense the absence of consistency. As a result, they are leery, discomforted, thus disabling you from being able to provide highly proficient CX.

I'm sensing some disbelief. Here's an example that will jog your memory. You got Random Restaurant A, right? Random Restaurant A is a family restaurant. So family oriented is this restaurant that it has a massive play area, video games, bright colors, Taylor Swift songs coming from the ceiling. Random Restaurant A is so family oriented that the Waltons and the Hustables would shed a tear walking through the front automatic doors. All possessing all the trappings of G ratings, the owner of this establishment could care less about kids and parents. Mr. Random Restaurant A is only concerned about the cash register and counting it at the end of the night. Mr. Random Restaurant A's legitimate goal is to be wealthy, not an altruistic goal to bolster familial relations in the world, not to be a moral pillar in the community. A "show me the money goal" with Brady Bunch trimmings is a raucously harsh mismatch. If you look at the restaurant closely you will find hidden gestures that express his thoughts and makes his authentic wishes known. It is found in his acts of maintaining his building and equipment in good condition, his attention to detail in keeping the place free from dirt. Ultimately, his true intention to act in a particular way will be discovered in his Cx and the type of Customer Server he hired, along with the Customer Servers appearance, their choice of words. The list goes on and on. Mr. Random Restaurant A's goals are blatantly obviously for someone looking for it.

Now, I'm aware that you don't have a goal marked by greed. Nevertheless, your true goal is apparent. So decide now what you want everyone to know about you through your product and CX and be harmonious in its implementation. Be regular, steady, and free from variation or contradiction. It will relieve your customers from the negative energy from lacking consistency. It will give them more zeal to patronize your product, thus strengthening your ultimate purpose.

In your attempts to create a Cx fingerprint, you must understand that there is absolutely no separating you from what you are selling. The fact that you are not the one at the front desk, or the one actually answering the phone, or the fact that your customers are unable to see you through your website does not detach you from your product or service. Your business is a snapshot of your heart for the community, and in some cases the world to see. It's an endorsement.

This is true as it relates to the Customer Sever that you hire. It's simple: if your business represents you, then the people representing your business represents you. The type of people and their inability or ability to present your vision, interpret your imagination and those of your customers are a proportionate representation of who you are. They are your avatar, ambassadors to your world. Your customers can easily draw conclusions about your personal life by the people that you have working for you.

I remember as a child, one of the most golden of the golden rules of my parents was: Do Not Misbehave In Public. My mother was, for the most part, an evenly keeled, soft spoken person. However, it wasn't unusual to see the full wrath of

God exacted through my mother if she felt our behavior was not fitting the public. She had this uncannily frightening ability to speak whole words and phrases through tightly clinched teeth. She could make a professional ventriloquist jealous. "Stop acting like you don't have home training!" or "You are behaving like you don't have a mother," would be her argument.

To my mother, our behavior in public pointed directly back to her and my father. It pointed back to our home and what goes on in private. In her mind, it labeled her children, our family. My parents worked too hard to allow the actions of two careless children to stain what they toiled to build and keep together. So, public behavior and speaking (articulations and vocabulary) were strictly enforced. My parents are good people. They love their children. They are fundamentally the salt of the earth and NOTHING should or WILL suggest otherwise-- not even their children.

It is not my attempt to compare your Customer Servers to children. But their behavior, like children, carries a heavier narrative, a narrative that describes and tells a story about you personally. Listless, rude, inattentive, people on your payroll, answering your phones, responding to your customer's needs says exactly what you feel about them and yourself. There's no differentiation. Honestly, are you able to separate Steve Jobs from Apple or Bill Gates from Microsoft? Doesn't the way they run their business from a public vantage point, give us some insight on who they are on personal level? I promise you; how they run their business is similarity to how they run their lives.

It's a profoundly serious topic. Do you ever ask yourself just how your favorite restaurant, your favorite clothing store feels about you? There is a quick and definite way to find out without even speaking with the owner of those businesses?

1. Notice the quality of Customer Server hired to facilitate your purchase.

2. Notice the quality of the product or service and time taken to develop the product or service.

3. The next time something goes wrong (as they always do) notice the level of urgency displayed to resolve the issue.
    a. How well did they listen
    b. How quickly did they come to a SUITABLE resolution? (SN: "Suitable Resolution" is defined by the unsatisfied customer not the vendor.)

    c. To what extent was the problem solved.

The answer to the above questions will give you perfect insight to the owner's opinion and affection for you.

Don't be fooled. Some companies are quick to point out that the store or company is franchised or privately owned. Therefore, the problem you are having does not reflect the brand or brand ownership. Have you seen those news reports where the local undercover news reporter goes in to a hotel and records horrible behavior by the staff? When the story is aired, the hotel brand has no comment except to say that the actions and behavior of the local property doesn't represent the brand as a whole? BULL HOCKEY! (Another technical term) It absolutely does! Every Hilton on earth is a reflection of Mr. Hilton himself. Every McDonald represents its stock holders, its corporate office, and everyone on McDonald's payroll. There's no separation.

I recently watched an episode of that reality show where the owner of a company goes undercover to promote, I mean, experience first-hand what his business and line employees are saying and doing. This episode featured an owner of a widely known what can easily be called low-end clothing store. This low-end clothing store has locations across the nation, situated in every impoverished neighborhood in America. Visit any hood or ghetto and you will find this clothing store. This store is far from being known as readily kept in cleanliness. Furthermore, it is certainly not known for hiring not-carney-like employees. One look at these employees and you will be convinced. "Yeah, she strangled a walrus before."

When the owner of these stores introduced himself, I was immediately struck with amazement that he wasn't engulfed by a cloud of flies and gnats. No one could have told me that the owner of those stores did not own a home directly beside Oscar the Grouch's trash can and or at least in a sewage drain. He was a good looking guy! By good looking I mean he was not horribly disfigured from birth like I would have imaged. He had an attractive wife. By attractive, I mean she was hot! He even had well-behaved children that weren't wearing state-issued electronic monitoring devices on their ankles. My judgment was way off.

The possession of those horribly erroneous thoughts of this guy and his personal life was no fault of my own. It was quite easy for me considering his business and the people he has representing his business. In a 2009 psychologist from Princeton University found that we make judgments about people based upon their warmth and competency. The favorable judgment is expressed toward individuals that seem warm and competent. Warmth and competency holds a considerable distance in space from the judgment I placed on the owner of the ghetto stores. His business contained neither of those characteristics, from the curb appeal all the way to the manner in which the clothes hung, or was tossed over the clothing rack. To form a positive appraisal of his business in my mind is a talent I don't have, easily aided by his CX. A deep concern about public opinion and being brand conscious is held by everyone. Only those of you who believe that portraying a positive image can affect not only your business but also you personal life. I guarantee you every slum lord's child is experiencing the reverberation from the public's disdain for their disgustingly unkempt, property devaluing hotel or apartment complex. I promise you if everyone knew you were the owner of the dilapidated, F-Rated restaurant on the corner, you would most likely receive some curious side-looks and gazes from the patrons in the grocery store where you shop. CX is a big deal. It's saying a lot about you. Do you know what it is saying? Do you like what is being said? Or do you care?

Having knowledge but lacking the power to express it clearly is no better than never having any ideas at all - Pericles

Make It Plain

In pursuit of the right CX for you, do not neglect quality: the extent to which your Customer Servers will or will not go to please your customers and the all-to-forgotten details. You are only distinguishable because of the details. Until you add details to any painting it's simply stylistic, impressionistic, blurry, abstract even. Anything without detail leaves too much to interpretation, perspective, and relativity. You want to control your narrative. Don't allow anyone to misconstrue your vision. Habakkuk chapter 2, verse 2: "And the LORD answered me, and said, Write the vision, and ***make it plain*** upon tables, ***that he may run that readeth it***." So, here's my Billy Graham moment. Apparently God, a Diety, the Universe, whatever you'd like to call this entity speaking to Habakkuk (Does the ability to pronounce Habakkuk serve as proof positive that there is a God?) gave him some important information. The importunate nature of the information can be found in the admonishment to "make it plain." Obviously there was a desire for clarity and an emphasis on quality of the delivery of the message. In the Jeff International Version of this scripture it interprets in this manner: "Hab, listen, dude, write down what I said. Don't use your normal illegible handwriting. Write it clearly, so that whoever reads it can understand." Had Habakkuk used short-hand, or not paid attention to detail the message would not have been delivered correctly. It goes further. "So that he may run that readeth it." The consequential nature of the message is also found the need for "he" to run. Why am I running to tell you something that isn't urgent? Ultimately the development of the message was important. Once the message was developed, it was necessary for whomever that read it to run. No need to run if the message was not clear. Which brings us back to "make it plain" or be detailed, don't take short cuts, don't leave room for interpretation.

My point is, your vision is important. The fundamental goal is for your customers to understand it, understand it so much so that they run and tell others about you. Your customer's ability to run is found in your ability to make it plain. Making it plain is accomplished by not forgetting details. Do not neglect the detail in pursuit of brand in Cx. To ensure your quality of CX is grade A you should ask yourself some questions.

It's not what we do once in a while that shapes our lives. It's what we do consistently. – Anthony Robbins

Is Your CX Unchanging?

Unchanging acts speaks to the nature of a person, place, or thing. The repetitive nature of a thing is what labels it or categorizes it. In the world of science, scientists have taught us that we can reach a specific conclusion and rest confidently about that conclusion if we experience the same results each time we set an action in to process. For instance, if we throw any object in to the air and it falls to the ground every time we try, it might be fair to say with assurance that what goes up must come down. Scientists have labeled actions that repeat themselves constantly Laws.

Believe it or not, based upon the frequency and/or infrequency in which your customers experience good or bad or excellent CX, a law has been derived about your product or service. Trip Advisor, one of the largest social media consumer advocate groups divvy's yearly the Trip Advisors Certificate of Excellence. This certificate is given to service-based businesses that ***Constantly*** produces positive feedback and comments on their sites – not to businesses that has one or two nice comments written about them; but the ones that insight an onslaught of positive customer commentary *on a consistent basis.* Just like scientists, Trip Advisors look for the reoccurrence of an action or result. From the frequency in which this action occurs the business is labeled and given an award of CX Excellence.

Once I held a position, something similar to an Area Manager. I say something similar because I possessed the office but not the title or pay. Anyway, I wasn't one of those AM's that emailed or announced by arrival. I believe we truly are who we are when we think no one is looking. At one property, we were struggling with our guest scores. Previously, I explained how certain brands require their properties to have a particular percentage of positive guest comments on a monthly basis. In other words, if 20 surveys were mailed out in a month, some brands require 80 to 85 percent to be returned with positive comments. This property was holding steady at 79, sometimes 65. I could not for the life of me figure out why. One night I decided to show up during peak check-in time to see what the guests are experiencing. I had a chance to speak to a guest that stayed for several nights on a weekly basis. She said: "I like staying here. You've got a good place. But, I tell ya, that gal in the mornings, she's a nightmare. If it wasn't for the locations being exactly what I need, I wouldn't stay here." She said, "I wrote about her attitude on Trip Advisor." I expressed my appreciation for her candor. I went directly from speaking to her to the manager's office and pulled up the hotel's website. Lo and behold, there it was, comment after comment about the property's GM. I didn't even read the full comments. The titles said it all:

"Manager Has A Bad Attitude." "Girl Working Desk Was Rude." "The Manager Told Me No!" "The Manager Came To Our Room And Yelled!" And on, and on, and on. I went to the brand website for guest comments, the same thing. Unbelievable! This manager had a personality that made Mr. T seem like Richard Simmons. Needless to say, I fired her. I actually mentioned that I would pay her to NOT work in the hotel business again.

The damage was almost insurmountable. The hotel was located in an office park. Myself and other corporate team members visited lost businesses in the local area with our hats in hand. We bought so many "I'm sorry lunches" that our bosses were not too pleased. We had to. Every office, totally independent of each other said the same thing. "Will 'Norma Bates' be there?" Some agreed to return. Some did not. One disgruntled office scolded us so badly that we felt we'd been sent to bed without dinner. She was no longer a fan. The mere fact that we allowed "Norma Bates" to operate in that manner as long as she did said something to her about our business in its entirety. She even contemplated discontinuing using the brand totally. What did we learn earlier? 96% of disgruntled guests say nothing about their negative experience. Of that 96, 91% will not return as a result. Nothing we said or did could convince her. Our hotel had been labeled in her mind, not because of one incident, but because of numerous occasions and constant bad experiences.

Something is reoccurring in your business, in your CX. What is it? Are you consistently blowing the minds of your patrons with memorable, genuine CX? Or, are you repeatedly dropping the ball, disappointing, discouraging, and creating unhappy customers on a continuous basis? From the answer of that question, your customers have scientifically labeled your business.

Being unique is better than

being perfect. -unknown

Is Your Cx Distinct?

JFK wrote: "Conformity is the jailer of freedom and the enemy of growth." You cannot afford to be the same as the others. If there are no distinguishing elements between you and your competitors then you are doomed to be lost in a sea of sameness. Let your amazing ability to create a memorable customer experience be your finger print, that which differentiates you from your competition.

Lets face it, everyone thinks they are nice. Have you ever met a Customer Server that was being rude and once you confronted them about it, they acknowledged their rudeness? "Excuse me, sir! You are really speaking to me in rude manner. I'm just calling to have my phone fixed." "Why, yes, you're right! I AM being rude. Please forgive me." THAT NEVER HAPPENS! Everybody thinks they're nice even when they are not being nice. Also, a person being simply cordial believes they are displaying the most explosive enthusiasm known to man. So, when you say that your CX is what differentiates you from the rest, it really doesn't. You must produce definitive, blaringly obvious CX characteristics that are not found any other place. The competition is nice. But, your team is nice and there's someone always present to open the door for the customer. Your competition is accommodating. Your team insists on carrying the purchased item out to the car. Your competition's website is user friendly. Your website issues a $1 credit toward each purchase every time someone logs on and buys something. Find your finger print.

Distinction starts with you. It doesn't matter if you own or manage a franchise. Your CX is different. Take for an example: You are an owner of a franchised grocery store. There's another grocery store of the same franchise 10 miles away. Same franchise, but I promise you two distinctly different stores. How? Because of you. You make your store totally unlike the other in nature and possibly quality. We are talking about a horse of different color. I'm saying your store is a special, totally dissimilar genome compared to the other guy—just by virtue of you being there. Your personalities are not the same. Your goals are not the same. Your outlook on life is not the same. Those distinguishing qualities are reflected in the way you approach your business which will attract a particular clientele as a secondary result. Do you have a favorite Starbucks? They are all the same supposedly. All the barristers are trained the same way. The same cup of coffee is being made at all the Starbucks in the world. Why do you favor one in particular? Your friendly regard is being shown to the Starbucks near your job as opposed to the one in walking distance from your house because it is reflecting a quality that you prefer. You make the difference. The finger print that you are attempting to make starts with you.

Don't be afraid to be you. It is the basis of your branding. It's what is recognizable about your business compared to the others. When I started my business I wanted who I am to proclaim flamboyantly, right down to the logo I chose and its colors. Yellow represents my desires of serving a beneficial or helpful purpose. I'm a friendly guy. It also represents my dynamic qualities. Indigo represents my sensitivity or attachment to spiritual values. Finally, there's the Sankofa Bird. Sankofa means to go back and get it. Ultimately, my desire as a business person is to be able to aid some of the people that have been neglected or feels that they were unable to obtain a chance in life. All of these qualities are represented in my logo, my brand. When you see my business you see me.

In life we develop particular likes and dislikes. Some of us grow up to be hyper sensitive about the environment. Others grow up and buy multiple SUV's. Who we are, truly, will make our success complete. When you decide who you are that decision becomes similar to an encasement around you. In your pursuit of success you are bouncing around like a pinball. You have a failure in your attempt for success here. You have a failure there. Just like a pinball you are being bumped and pushed away. Until you find a slot that fits YOU. When you fall in to the joint that best fits and benefits you, success comes in droves. Because you stayed true to whom you are, and did not transform yourself to meet demand, or the market. You are now more able to operate in the success comfortably because you are operating as YOURSELF. What's easier than being yourself? The same pinball action happens when a person changes themselves to be successful quickly. Unfortunately, however, they are unable to experience the fullness of success because they must behave unnaturally, totally unlike when you wake up morning after morning to go to work to be what nature has created you. Your distinction starts with you. There is not another you. Let your goals, your desires, your ambitions be the foundation of your CX. Your CX should be the reflection of what you are trying to say to the world.

I wasn't real quick, and I wasn't real strong. Some guys will just take off and it's like, whoa. So I beat them with my mind and my fundamentals. Larry Bird

Is Your Cx On Target?

Do you accomplish the goal? What is your business providing? What service is being offered? Why are customers going to your website? Once you answer that question, answer this one? Are your customers getting what they expecting on a base level? You have a website that sells books. Are your customers actually getting the book? You have a car detailing business. Are the vehicles clean when the customer leaves? I know this question seems ridiculous. But, you can have the nicest Customer Server in the world but if the customer isn't getting fundamentally what they want, your CX is worthless.

Your customers come for your product. The experience while retrieving that product is what makes them return customers. If they can't get your product for whatever reason (phone busy, website frequently down, constantly defective products) then these issues render your great customer service worthless.

Being consistent, being on target, being distinct are just the fundamentals. If you don't have these three areas covered, you are a joey in a cage of hungry wolves. In America we have been told that we can make our dreams come true if we work hard. There are thousands of people that have taken this saying to heart. There are thousands of people seeking to be successful in your industry alone. Only the strong survives.

Target #1 Find Your Sweet Spot

Finding the appropriate Cx for you is actually like going on a mission to find oneself. You are not like the store down the street. Don't try to be. There is actually a special corner in the world of CX carved just for you. No one else is able to fill that spot except you. You have to figure where that carving is.

I've opened numerous hotels. I've had to revamp a few opened ones too. A lot of the decisions concerning a new hotel are predicated upon the market or the competition – at least in the beginning. Initially, I spy on what the surrounding comparable hotels are doing and I position the hotel closely similar to them. What happens in the long run, the hotel begins to develop on its own. It begins distinguishing itself from the rest. Once the hotel has found its own identity, I begin to either lower or raise our rates to pull out from the pack. You have to listen to your business. Pay close attention to the type of clientele and their wants, the type of Customer Server and their wants, your market and its wants, even your competitors and their wants. In doing so, you will find your sweet spot.

One day as I was exiting the front entrance to go to my car, a guest was entering at the same time. It was habitual for me: I smiled; I said something to garner a smile or a small laugh. "Welcome weary traveler! Come and rest thine weary eyes." I held door for the gentleman and went about my merry way.

Probably a week or so later, I was viewing the comments posting on our guest comment website. I noticed that someone had scored us a 5 Star. His comment was that the hotel was very clean, the staff was wonderful, and the breakfast was great. The manager even held the door for me when I arrived." Boing! Up went my antennae. Guess what I started doing, especially on high volume nights and high volume hours? I stood by the door and opened it for every guest that I could. Just doing so lifted our average score for the week 10 points and we ended the month significantly higher in Guest Services Scores than we anticipated.

What is the lesson to be learned from this?

1. Listen to your Customers. They will tell you what they like and don't appreciate. Often we shy away from bad comments especially those on the internet. We feel the comments do not represent the hard work we expend on a daily basis. Also, when it comes to posting comments on the internet, its ten times easier to get a response when we make a mistake than it is when we are wonderful and performing well. Good comments or not, take them seriously. They are your window in to finding that sweet

spot that will produce constant good comments and better reputation online.

2. When you do receive favorable comments, repeat those actions. It's called the "kicking the leg" method. Rover knows how tell us just when we are performing actions that he likes. He wags his tail. When he is overjoyed, he kicks his legs franticly, reveling in the moment. And you know what? Every time those actions are done, Rover gives us the same reactions. Well, you need to scratch around your business, create best practices that have your customers "kicking their legs" reveling in your CX. Don't treat positive comments just as a moment to celebrate. See them as Rover kicking his leg. Repeat those actions as much as possible. Eventually, your Customers will lick your face in appreciation. (Not really, I hope.)

3. Once the sweet spot has been found, those actions need to be made mandatory-emboldened by posting pink posted notes about your team members area, threatening punishment, as result of breaking this rule, by firing squad or being force fed Chinese food and then removing all bathroom stalls. They should become best practices and

taught to every existing Customer Server and all future ones. Once again, we are back to our friend Habakkuk. You have to make it plain to your Customer Servers. They must understand first of all the importance of the "kicking leg" action – "kicking leg" means happy customer, which means more money, or at least a sense of financial ease to facilitate payroll. Most (I say most, not all) Customer Server shortcomings from lack of training, lack of fully understanding the training or simply lack of information. Remember, like Habakkuk, you want the person learning your vision to run, to be excited, and to have an uncontrollable sense of urgency. That is not possible if the vision is not made plain.

Target #2- Reward Your Do Gooders

For those of us whose livelihood is predicated upon the success of others, you should really appreciate those individual that brings you closer and closer to success. I don't mean those team members that occasionally inch you close to success. I mean those team members that constantly perform at a high level, those team members that always cast a positive light on your business, product, and service. Those Team Members get it. And they should be rewarded for it frequently.

Why reward high-performing Customer Servers:

1. They remove a significant amount weight off of your shoulders. You can't be everything to everybody. You can't wear all the hats. You have to relinquish at least one of your hats to your team. Imagine having to perform every duty necessary to keep your business running. The pronunciation and definition of the words bed, relaxation, and personal time would be etched from your brain permanently. Your life is hectic as it is. If you did not have your team, it would be overwhelmingly worse. They

should be appreciated in some way for those infrequent sighs of relief you have, at the very least.

2. The trustworthy, proven Customer Server appreciates you and your product or service as much as you do. They take your business seriously. They've captured your vision. Made it part of their own. And, both of you are attempting to capture success together. The high performing Customer Server has personalized your business. They should be reward just for seeing things from your vantage point.

3. The Huffington Posting wrote the following in a 2016 article about unhappy, unappreciated team members: *"Sales people will not work as hard to upsell, close deals and rebut those that turn down an offer."* Also: *"their loyalty to the brand they are employed with decreases. They are less likely to back their company and only offer neutral commentary."*

Frequently rewarding team members often translates in to better treatment of your customers. There is a straight line drawn from an unhappy customer that extends directly to the unhappy Customer Server. Then the line extends to his or her compensation and positive or negative reinforcement by the department head or executive. Cause a chain reaction. Reward your high performer. It will cause a crescendo that will eventually affect your customer.

Target #3 Customer Retention

Listening when someone is freely volunteering information is easy. What do you do when you have to pursue the information you need to find your sweet spot. As a young man, I held a small penchant for "playing the field." I started dating a young lady whilst already in the full throws of another relationship. I held each young lady at bay from making acquaintances for a considerable amount of time, but not forever unfortunately. I received a phone call (at work mind you) from one of the young lady's best friend. She was, I assume, making her case as to my worthlessness. I really couldn't understand what she was saying because her voice was distorted through the phone from her yelling. Eventually the yelling ceased. I asked to speak to my girlfriend #2. She picked up the receiver, noticeably hurt. It was more than apparent that she was destroyed. Through her weeping she ventured in to the now well-established game of insulting me. At an uncomfortably and extremely later moment, she got around to asking what I considered at the moment a significantly valuable question. "Why didn't you tell me you already had a girlfriend?" Now in my twenties, like most infants, my brain was still forming. I scraped my brain to find the best answer that I could find. After a second I'd found one. I told her knowing full well that the response about to fall from my lips was as lame as President Clinton's excuse. With an audible smurk, I said: "You didn't ask." Click! Never heard from her again. Lesson to be learned; asking questions is a good thing.

Did you know that 50% of all complaints go unreported? For reasons that range from fear to doubt, a large portion of our customers have chosen not to report the problem or negative experience. 50% is a tremendously large and frightening number. It doesn't stop their friends. Not only are you out of the loop with a significant number of your customer's opinion of you, but according to Right Now Customer Experience Impact Report, 90% of disgruntled customers stop doing business after having a negative experience. 90%! These silent but angry customers are dangerous for your success. They're like CO_2. There's absolutely no sign of their threat. The next thing you know, your business is dead. And you're left wondering, confused like a 10 year old on Jeopardy. What did I do wrong? I have a great product; my CX is excellent. What am I doing wrong? The answer, my friend, is you're not resolving the issue soon enough.

How do you resolve a customer's problem rapidly? Well the answer to that question is different predicated upon what type of business you have. An internet business is totally different compared to a brick and mortar business. But, the one thing that is constant in both is that you have to develop some way to get your customers to talk to you. Resolving the issue as soon as it happens or shortly thereafter is crucial to diminishing that illusive 50% that is quietly suffocating your business. You have to derive a way to ask the customer about their experience shortly after purchase or fulfillment of service.

"How was everything" is not enough anymore. In CX the experts have convinced us that manipulating our customers is ok. The experts have taught us to say "No" without actually saying the word "No." They've taught us indirect ways to ask questions. Personally, I think those methods are a crock of bull. When the issue is as pertinent as losing customers, customers that we now know have chosen not to inform you of their negative experience, but are highly likely not to return and even more likely to inform others of their distaste for your product or business, I don't think that there's much room to be subliminal or vague. You need to ask the exact question. "Did you experience anything while shopping with us that would deter you from returning?" "Did we disappoint you in anyway?" "What did we do wrong?" "How can we be better?" You need to feel the urgency of getting your customers to share their experience. You need 12 positive experiences to recover from one negative, according to Parature. Resolving the issue ASAP must be the goal. Because once the ball is rolling, it is really difficult to get it back.

What is the purpose of brands? It is used to make you distinguishable. Along with the word distinguishable, I like to use the word recognizable. Why would you want to be recognizable? Being recognizable makes it easier for someone who is making a concerted effort to find you. Ok, in the path of branding your CX you have decided who you are, you are making your vision plain, not neglecting the details. You've found your sweet spot. Now every customer that walks in to your facility leaves barefoot because you not only knock their socks off, their shoes disintegrate in the white-heated awesomeness of your CX. There are high-fives, chest bumping, and rap-dude hand gestures all around. You have made a convert, a loyal follower, a groupie. How do you treat your minions? How do you facilitate CX as it relates to customer retention?

You know that store that you frequent? I would imagine that the owner of the business enjoys the relationship you've established. As in any relationship, especially mutually beneficial ones, it stands to reason that both participating parties demonstrate their appreciation for the relationship with gifts and/or surprises. You've been going to the same barber since your childhood. You spend as much time at the neighborhood coffee shop as you do in church. Many of the places you spend your hard-earned dollars have stopped calling you Mr. or Mrs. They have become so familiar that your first name suffices. How has those businesses demonstrated their affection toward you? Janet Jackson asked the questions significantly better than I: "What Have You Done For Me Lately?"

Listen, you probably have learned by now. If you haven't, let me teach you. Money doesn't grow on trees. For a lot of us, money barely produces itself on pay day. Something else you might know, the economy is not the healthiest for us on the bottom rung. For many, it has its foot over the grave and the other on a banana peel doused in motor oil. Business owners are aware of this financial hardship. Heck, many of them are struggling too. This brings me to my point. Why doesn't your favorite dress shop appreciate you in some way, realizing that you are forking over your hard-earned cash? Why doesn't your online book store have record of your monthly book purchase and make a suggestion once in a while instead of having you wonder from isle to isle like a mouse in a labyrinth. Why don't they express their gratitude in some way, realizing you are a monthly staple, like a t-shirt with the store's logo, like: "Here Mr. Staton, a cool pin for your loyalty." It only has 30 seconds worth of ink it. But, we think it's' the thought that count." It's simple. There are customers and then there are return customers, frequent flyer, frequent stayer, loyal patrons. These are people who have found profound worth in a business, in a product -- so much so that they've etched out time in their busy schedule to add them. That business is a part of their routine, a part of their lives. Many are picking up their dry cleaning before they pick up their children.

Here are the hard facts:

1. According to Bain and Co: "increasing customer retention (focusing on your existing customers) by 5% will increase

profits by 25 to 95%." Dude, 25 - 95%! Need I say more? I will.

2. Most companies will hire a team of talented sales people who will spend countless dollars on marketing to acquire new customers. Bain and Co. found that customer acquisition costs 6 times more than simply making your existing customers happy. Dude, it costs you 6 times more to pick up new customers than to keep existing ones happy! Need I say more? I will.

3. According to Market Matrix: new customers are only 20% likely to make a purchase. Existing customers are 70% more likely to purchase from you. Dude! 70%! And, yes there's more.

4. Existing customers are likely to purchase 33% more than a new one. Dude (never mind you get the picture)

It just makes sense doesn't it? What has your relationship done for you lately? If the answer is nothing, you should seriously re-think that relationship. A frequent purchaser such as you, as we learned, spends more and cost less. Appreciating you is just good business and IS good CX.

Chapter 3

To Be Or Not To Be In Cx

You've created your brand of CX. It reflects you and all the things you desire the public to know. What do you do now? First, you need to recognize that your brand of CX is precious. It is rare, and it's the foundation to success. Secondly, you need to maintain its status or integrity from damage or destruction. In this chapter we will be discussing ways of protecting your brand of CX. We will go over frequent mistakes made by Customer Servers and executives in the administration of CX.

Be Preventive

Shhh, listen! Do you here it? There is a considerable amount of discourse happening in your business. This chatter is your business informing you what it needs to be successful. From its location to the type of clientele, your business is explaining to you what you and it needs. Only those with sensitive ears are able to hear it. It's up to you to develop the ear that can hear the conversation. Further, it's up to you to know how to respond to what your business is saying. With certain locations come a particular clientele. With a particular clientele come particular demands or wants, needs and potential problems. You must be intimately knowledgeable of all of these things to be able to help bring about excellent CX. As it relates to the potential problems, they must be addressed before they happen. Imprudent does not come close to being the appropriate word to describe a person that is reactionary, handling issues only when they happen. At that point, it's too late. And based upon the incident and the Customer's level of disappointment, there's a 50% chance that the actions you take to make the situation better will actually be what the Customer wants. On top of all that, 50% of all customers don't tell you when they've been disappointed. They just quietly suffer their disappointment, like a CO_2 leak. Next thing you know, your business is being mourned, laid to rest, and eulogized.

Shielding or maintaining the integrity of your Cx is a time sensitive issue. Consequentially a Customer Sever must be preemptively strategic. Correcting problems when they happen is called a delayed reaction. If you know your business attracts a large amount of kids on the weekends. Your business is telling you:

a) The noise level will probably be heightened
b) All the trash produced in the day will mostly like NOT make it to the trash cans.

c) Those patrons without children will be slightly bothered by the melee.

Knowing these things, you should strategize on how to combat these issues. When I was GM, the summer with its warm sun, and blue skies caused the hibernating beasts I called *"The Inattentive Parent"* to awaken. The Inattentive Parent would wake from its winter slumber, gather all their cubs and proceed to cause havoc on unsuspecting airplane passengers, hotel guests, and all summer attraction visitors. These Inattentive Parents feel that by virtue of having more than one child, the necessity to control the volume of their children's voices, their children's tendency to run in halls, and their children's tendency to yell while in the hotel rooms diminishes. And all being discomforted by their wake must understand that they are children and "children will be children."

We prepared for Inattentive Parent season three months prior to its arrival. We pre-blocked the arrivals of all Inattentive Parents. We place them all together so they can run each other crazy, away from unsuspecting guests. We implemented and strictly enforced quiet hour. We had all the Inattentive Parents to sign an agreement that they will adhere to quiet hour. We placed a huge teddy bear at the end of each hall that held a laminated sign. Each year the sign would have different nauseating bear puns like; "I can bearly stay awake," or "It's time forest." (It's time for rest) These were all tactics implemented because we listened to what the business told us.

You know, as a lingerie website, that your traffic will peak on Valentine's Day and months when there's a lot weddings. Months prior to these events you need to be greasing up the cogs of our website to ensure it doesn't crash. Also, it would be prudent to have a lot of items in the color red. And lastly, par levels and inventory to meet demand would be something you would want to visit prior to the dates when people tend to go scantily clad.

There needs to be ongoing creative, concise and preventive meetings and conversations about how to offer genuine Customer Service and how to avoid mishaps. All responsible Customer Servers should be required to offer different suggestions. Our Customer Servers are on the frontlines. They experience the Customers firsthand. They are aware of their patterns, the questions being asked on a daily basis, the areas of successes and the areas where there is less success. Customer Servers have been educated by the customer. As a result, the Customer Server should be able, with some ease, to create strategies and offer ideas to combat possible mistakes based upon the information/intelligence received from the Customers. These strategies should be implemented as part of a routine in every interaction with the Customer.

Be Engaged Not Just Nice

There's a massive chasm between being nice and being engaged. Being nice is to being engaged as paper airplanes are to Lear Jets or Mr. Bean is to 007. You expect the person next to you at the stop light to be nice. A Customer Servers needs to be more. You won't find a lot of engaged Customer Servers. Mostly, the extent to which most Customer Servers are invested is the extent to which their direct deposit is on time. In order to be engaged you must have an invested interest or personal regard for the business, your product, your customers. This interest must be linked to a personal tie possessed by the Customer Server in your business. In other words, an engaged Customer Server is personally invested. To them your product reflects them; your success is their success. From this personal involvement comes a heightened facilitation of CX. Engaged or personally involved Customer Servers will be people who aren't just smiling, seeming happy, and quasi-pleasant. They are people who like a heat seeking missile are searching for opportunities to blow the minds of your customers, people who like a radar are noticing dots on the map or patterns and reacts to them. An engaged Customer Server will notice a Customer with a cast on their arm or leg and relay this information in order that a sympathy card could be mailed soon thereafter. They will conduct qualifying conversations with your guests to obtain further information to make the transaction better or even obtain further opportunities for future service.

Once at a coffee house my wife and I frequented, the server came over to our table and said to my wife: "I noticed the type of coffee you order. Would you mind trying this? It's somewhat similar to yours." My wife tried it and it automatically became her favorite coffee drink. In this same coffee house, the manager would call my wife and me to the front of the line, no matter how many people were waiting before us. Without asking, make our drinks and allow us to sit down and he would retrieve payment for the drinks when they were not busy. That's engaged. They remembered our faces, our drinks, and knew us well enough to defer payment. That's CX on a different level. I mean, my wife and I went sometimes just to see how many people we could jump in line. It was wonderful.

Being engaged protects the Cx you've created because you've hired a Customer Server that can connect on two fronts on a personal level: your product and customer. They are connected to your product because they are invested in you, your business, and your vision. They are connected to the customer because they are honed in on the customer's wants and needs. To find an engaged Customer Server may mean that you may have to be a little strategic in your hiring. It may mean that you hold the position open a little long you would like until you find the right Customer Server. Once you have that Customer Server on board that will "Tim The Tool Man Taylorize" your CX, you will realize that the wait was worth it.

Be Cost Effective

Customer Service translates in to dollars lost and gained. Monthly, after a concise review of the P&L and Balance Sheet, there needs to be a conversation equally concise about the increase or decrease of Customer satisfaction and retention. It really doesn't matter if you have a landscaping business. When you submit your invoice, submit along with it a small survey asking the customer to critique your service. Ask to include how they feel they've been treated the last month. You own a hair salon? While the customer is waiting under the dryer, give them an I-Pad that has a CX survey loaded and have them critique you.

Joe Causon, CEO of the Institute of Customer Service says: *"Good customer service is highly prized. It is clear that most customers want a balance between customer service and price. But about a quarter (23 per cent) of purchasers said that they would pay more – on average an additional 10 per cent – in return for a better customer experience"* Do you understand what that means? Twenty-three percent of your customers will pay up to 10% more for your product or service simply because you are willing to treat them nicely, to be engaged, to anticipate their needs. Can your bottom line use a 10% increase this year? Yes, it can. (I'll answer for you)

It's expensive to provide bad Customer Service. Look at this equation: The salary or wage expense for the horrible Customer Server + capacity costs + the 50% of customers that are talking badly about your business + your personal expenses = a significant amount of unnecessary cash outflow. You have enough expenses that are innate to having a business. The more you eliminate non-essential liabilities and expenses the more money you save.

Bad Customer Service is like a leaking boat. You would never board a leaking ship. You would never purchase a leaky ship. You should never be the captain of a leaking ship. That Customer Server with a sharp tone, the unpleasant voice, the snobbish attitude is a leak in your ship. Their salary is making your ship weaker and weaker. You don't know it, but you are slowly sinking financially. The labor expense to that bad Customer Server is literally paying to piss your customers off. Every time you sign the paycheck of that bad Customer Server you are rewarding them for the demise of your company.   Get rid of unnecessary expenses.

I've worked with clients who would rather give their first born than to give money back or give an irate customer something for free. Don't get me wrong. It's totally understandable. Money feels better when it's in your hand. Money looks better when it's in your bank account. When you have to take the money out of your hand or bank account and give it to someone, it causes considerable discomfort. The consequences, however, of not exhausting all methods to resolve customer problems are dire. It is actually more expensive to lose a customer than it is to refund or offer a free peace offering.

Your business requires the obtaining of new customers and the retaining of current ones to function. The potentiality of retaining and obtaining lives in the facilitation of CX for the customer you presently have. Within every current customer's experience lies the possibility or prohibition of future customers. Also, the level of astonishment or disappointment experienced by your CX will dictate the extent to which the customer will promote or obstruct. Years ago the saying was, for every 1 disgruntled customer 20 will be negatively affected. That was the old days. Today, because of social media, 1 disgruntled customer can easily affect 1 million in one day. The importance of correcting Cx mistakes, with respect to its power to produce a negative effect on future customers and doing so prior to the customer leaving or logging off, exist in a high degree. Knowing this, how senseless is refusing a refund compared to the capability of losing the current and future customers developing into actuality? It is ultimately less expensive to give money back.

Your expenses to capture new customers far exceed the cost of customer retention. If you convert the time expended apologizing, addressing negative comments on social media, writing letters, and coaching team members in to dollars, and compares it to what you spent on getting it right the first time or resolving the issue when it happens, you will notice that the two are markedly different.

The goal is to get it right the first time. And if offering a refund will make them happy then by all means do so. The cost of not making them happy far exceeds the expense of the refund. Remember, you've created a new entity, your Cx. You've pretty much put yourself on the line publicly. You have to do what it takes to make sure you cover yourself from negative exposure. You can handle what's in front of you. Once it's gone, it can morph into a creature unimaginable. Protect your CX by solving the issue immediately.

It's Alright To Be Not Right

You know what strips you naked of the protection you have worked so hard to develop around your CX? Arguments. Like in an exposed secret, arguing with the customers removes everything protecting your CX, exposing something no one wants to see. Once I was training a group of hotel front desk team members on the proper way to make a reservation. We were performing LIVE training or actually receiving calls for reservations when a gentleman called to make a reservation. I took the call and proceeded to demonstrate the techniques. One of the major components to making a reservation is at the end of the call always recite to the guest all that was discussed during the call. I repeated the day of arrival, the name of the arriving guest, discussed the type of room, and finished the call with my usual "Will there be any other questions that I could answer or do you need any further assistance?" The caller said "No." And we hung up.

Ironically this gentleman arrived on a day when we were training on proper ways to check-in a guest. The gentleman arrived at the desk with a smile. He read my name tag and said, "Jeff, you took my reservation." He gave me his name. I searched for his name. I could not find it. I performed a wider search for his name and found that he was scheduled to arrive for another date. I apologized and said: "I'm sorry, I have you arriving on a different date." He emphatically denied that his reservation was for the future date. He believed I made a mistake and I was wrong. I needed to fix it. Again, it is procedure in making a reservation to recall all of the info back to the guest before hanging up. I know I had done this. Instead of arguing the point, I accepted responsibility for "*the mistake*," apologized profusely and upgraded him for his troubles. Remember, I was not wrong; plus, I had 5 trainees watching the entire exchange.

This topic harkens back to a topic we discussed earlier, Keeping your Cx Zones Sterile. Before you enter any place where a sale or customer experience can be affected you must destroy the existence of the need to be right. A Customer Server that possesses the need to be right is a Customer Server bound for failure. It doesn't matter if the customer is spewing words that make no sense, reciting rules that have nothing to do with you, your business, or your product. The Customer Server should never attempt in any way to prove the customer wrong. All attempts should be focused on a resolution to the problem. If I had a dime for every time a guest walked in to my hotel with a coupon for a totally different hotel, I would have the money of an Arab king. There were instances when guests would walk up to the desk brandishing a coupon offering from 20 - $50 off a standard room and then demand an additional AAA or AARP discount. You tell someone over 60 years old they can't have their senior discount. You tell someone that has spent numerous years in Iran, Iraq, and Afghanistan that they can't have their military discount. I promise you, my friend, you are asking for an emotionally heightened moment.

You know all the esoteric comings and goings of your business. You know that normally Saturday and Sundays are your high volume times; and thus, discounts are discontinued. You know that 8am until noon are the windows for senior discounts. You know that the 40% off sales applies to the items that are out of season. Your customers aren't aware of these rules. They just want to patronize your product that displays a price point that is attractive to them. The lawyer clauses and fine print disclosures are not concerns for your customers. There are no absolutes in CX. Most customers read the fine print and know to ask "Ok, what's the catch?" There are those who really believe that the commercial touting the blow-out sale on men suits and dress pants include the imported Italian Armani suites, shoes, tie and socks.

Once you've informed the customer that they were wrong in their assumptions and they give you heated verbal kickback, it is not your job to commence to yelling like Tom Cruise in "A Few Good Men." It is your job to realize the existence of a discontented customer. You should automatically remember that 1 unhappy customer can negatively affect 1 million. Also remember that in every current or present customer lays the capability to promote or obstruct other customers, and begin to scour your brain to bring about a reasonable resolution. It is a solution you want not to be right.

Department heads, this will not be an easy road to hoe for you. I've had numerous of talented Customer Servers that quit because they felt I did not "have their back" or support them in their efforts to prove the customer wrong. Once, I managed an extended stay type hotel – one of those hotels that only rent weekly and monthly. This type of facility left the majority of the housekeeping to the tenant. If the tenant was renting monthly, housekeeping was only bi-weekly. One tenant, one day, not really knowing what month it was let alone what day, decided to verbally assault the front desk team and housekeeping team about not having any housekeeping in over a month. The executive housekeeper contacted me. Instructed me to hurry to where she was because there was a guest displaying some threatening tendencies. When I arrived on the floor, you could hear the angry guest from the stairwell. He stood in his door shirtless, waving past receipts that, in his opinion, proved that he had been stiffed on housekeeping on several occasions. This gentleman was cursing, hitting the wall, calling the housekeeping executive unsavory names—not a happy camper. When I began speaking to him my first mission was to calm matters, get him to lower the volume of his voice and stop using threatening behavior and words. I listened to him. He gave me his receipts; all covered with what I assumed was dirt and oil. I feigned my interest and understanding of the receipts. After a few months the receipts are just a mess. I paged through his precious receipts, like: "Hmmm, hmm. Uhmmm, Uhmmm, ok, hmmm." Then suddenly I said, "I see the problem. Mr. X, let me take care of this." I told the housekeeper to clean his room. "We are putting you on a new schedule, Mr. X for your trouble."

Now, the executive housekeeper was nowhere near happy about the resolution. "Mr. Jeff, why did my girls have to clean that man's room? You know he was wrong!" I responded: "It's not about being right. He's a paying guest. We need to make sure we don't lose him." "But, Mr. Jeff, he called me a name!" I responded: "I explained to him that verbally abuse will not be tolerated." She returned: "If that had been your wife, you would have responded differently." I said: "Not at all." I lost a good executive housekeeper that day. She felt I didn't stand up for her and her team. In all honesty, the guy was full of gator dung. It wasn't his day for housekeeping. I was not going to further allow this situation to plummet in to additional abysmal pits of hell by breaking out forensic evidence to prove him wrong. I wasn't interested in who was right. I was interested in a resolution.

It will be difficult to find Customer Servers that are willing to thwart all tendencies to be right, to be wrong when they are 100% right. Being wrong diminishes us in some way. We feel defeated, less than. This can be overcome by having a particular type of personality, and having confidence, topics we will get in to in depth the next chapter.

The bottom line is, your "rightness" is nothing to protect. Your CX is. Arguments are only two people vying to be right. You can replace the words spoken in every argument with the words "I'm right and you're wrong" and the essence of the argument would not be lost. You are a Customer Server. You are not hired to be right. You are hired to fulfill the needs of the customer. Pursuing or protecting your "rightness" makes you a gatekeeper, sworn to protect all that is inside the gate. Casting away the desire to be right and even allowing yourself to be wrong, makes you a skilled agent of the customers' needs and their experience.

Don't Be Afraid

You are the next Donatella Versace, right? You have so much confidence in your fashion designs that you opened a store in the trendy part of downtown. You have a lot of confidence in your product and your store. However, you don't feel quite as sure on how to attract people to your store. You see your neighboring store mates outside on the side walk stopping people and talking to passersby. You know you have to participate in that type of aggressive advertising. But you can't. Every now and then you have a customer or two to venture through your doors. You watch them peruse your shelves and racks, but the final result is always that sound of the tingling bell hanging on your door indicating the customer is leaving. You know if you walk up to the customer and introduce yourself and make suggestions it would increase the likelihood of purchase. But you can't. You are too afraid.

When we were cave people and words were more guttural and more befitting for when someone hits you in the face, when we chased and caught animals that were just as likely to eat us as we were to eat them, when life itself was literally predicated upon what we accomplished on daily basis, there wasn't too much fear around. In my opinion, fear was only meant to make us aware of danger, an indicator that: "Hey, maybe you should tread lightly when you go in to unfamiliar places." Apart from life threatening occasions, fear really doesn't have any place in our world. I can hear people right now: "Jeff, fear keeps me from jumping off the Empire State Building." Fear shouldn't do that, intelligence should. In the times when we should be participating in actions that would benefit us, often fear trumps intelligence.

You can create the most remarkable CX known to man; but, if your Customer Server is fearful, you are weakening your protection. A really soft spoken phone operator in your Cx help line, a person at your information desk that won't look at anyone in their eyes, a stuttering representative visiting clients, all indications of fear. These people may be the salt of the earth, able to quote early 19th century poetry, able to quote the Canterbury Tales verbatim. These are attributes that would possibly dazzle your customers or clients, but are of no consequence if they can't overcome shyness.

Forrest Gump taught us eloquently: "Life is like a box of chocolates. You never know what you're gonna get." It is this lack of knowing that frightens us. Fear demonstrates a lack of confidence, confidence in yourself, in your team, in your product or service. In the darkness of customer service you encounter all type of personalities. You never know what type of customer will come next. Well, Pythagoras (a great 5th century philosopher) taught us to obtain what we don't know by what we know. What we know is called a "Given." What are the Givens in CX? One given is your product or service. You must obtain the confidence with dealing with customers from knowledge that you have a remarkable product. You are offering something that will benefit the public. Let the confidence in what you are offering be the light in the darkness that is customer service.

You can do this. You are more than capable to weather all that entails being a Customer Server. You are not a "fly-by-night" business owner. You are not just some warm body behind a desk. You are not just a voice on the other end of the line. Your website is not just another place for ecommerce in a sea of internet gimmicks. The Given is You! The Given is your product. The Given is your Service. These alone will make you successful. Don't doubt. Don't be afraid. You will succeed.

The list goes on and on about things that could frighten us in customer service. Don't be paralyzed by them.

Don't Be Sarcastic

Recently, I was assigned to a hotel in Wisconsin. The prior owners of the property defaulted on their financial responsibilities and the courts rewarded my company receivership. When I take over new hotels (or newly assigned hotels) I like to dress in everyday clothes, nothing professional, something more suitable for Starbucks not hotel management. When I arrive, before I ask to meet the manager, I like to talk with the Guest Service Representative (GSR): ask questions about the hotel, the area, etc. This particular time the GSR was slightly different.

I approached the front desk and greeted the gentleman behind the counter. He was really busy, apparently cleaning his work area because he barely acknowledged me and returned a half-hearted "hello."

I continued: "Are you booked tonight?" This was apparently a peculiar question because he stopped cleaning long enough to look around the lobby, then the parking lot (both of which were empty) and said: "If I get any busier, I'll have to get some help," clearly indicating that I should have derived the answer to my question from the inactivity in the lobby and parking lot.

"How are you rooms?" I said. With an "almost smile" that would make Mona Lisa look like Magic Johnson, he replied: "Nice?"

It was apparent that this gentleman enjoyed his talent for sarcasm. Had I been a real customer his actions would have caused me to take my business elsewhere. Webster defines sarcasm as "a sharp ironic utterance designed to cut or give pain; language that is usually directed against an individual." I think a portion of that definition bears repeating: "...language used AGAINST an individual." Simply said, sarcasm is language used as a weapon. The Greek root "sarkazein" means to tear the flesh like dogs." LIKE DOGS, PEOPLE!

The Smithsonian wrote an article in 2011 called "The Science Of Sarcasm? Yeah, Right!" They found that "sarcastic statements are sort of a true lie... the communication works as intended if you're listener gets that you're being insincere." For the record, insincerity has no place in CX.

I'm spending a considerable amount of time with this topic because sarcasm has become a badge of honor nowadays. There are very few people that don't describe themselves as sarcastic. I call it the "Chandler Binging" of conversations. The title obviously derived from the hit sitcom "Friends" and the character Chandler Bing. Chandler was the master of predatory sarcasm, from the words he chose right down to the inflection or intonation used. He would ravage anyone with his passive aggressive sarcastic manner. In a way, Chandler popularized being sarcastic. The Smithsonian wrote: "Sarcasm so saturates the 20th century... phrases has almost lost their literal meaning."

Let me be clear, sarcasm, despite its popularity, has no place in CX. It is supposedly a sign of a quick wit and heightened intellect. It is really a sign of a person displaying their superiority, marking territory. This is totally unacceptable.

I promise you, detecting a person with a predatory penchant for sarcasm will be easy. Like bacon strips wrapped around a pork chop, they have themselves wrapped around themselves. They lay in wait to demonstrate their sarcastic wit. It does however mean, once again, that you be more selective with your hiring process. On your applications ask questions like: describe your sense of humor? Who was your favorite "Friends" character? If any of the answers leans toward sarcasm, place their application in a waste basket labeled: "Hell-To-The-No." I'm not being so Spartan, in that I want to dictate or marshal someone's personality. Definitely, carry any personality that makes you feel comfortable in this world. Understand though, sarcasm belongs nowhere near CX.

When customers ask for our help, they are admitting a modicum of helplessness, a level of weakness or inability. Asking for help is another way to say "I can't." So, being sarcastic or "tearing the flesh like a dog," when our customers come to us for help, when our customers are saying, in essence "I can't," makes the Customer Server a predator, an opportunist, unfit to represent your product or service-- a sure fire way to close your doors. And I'm sure that's exactly what you need. Yeah, right!

Signs Of a Good Customer Sever

Be Yourself

With the ramped outbreak of Post Traumatic Purchasing Syndrome (PTPS) that our customers have, we now know that genuine CX is the only cure for this sickness. Customer service is not easy. There's certainly a level of skill involved to be successful with dealing with the public. In my travels, I've trained numerous of people how to connect, how to interact, how to be pleasing. In doing so, I've received my share of kick-back and recalcitrance from unwilling team members. I've been told: "Jeff, that's just not Me." or "Jeff, I can't act that way. Ima keep it real." One of the largest misconceptions about CX is that your personality is not enough, that you have to pretend to be someone else. Just not true. Be yourself, but an enhance version. Some interprets being an enhanced version of you as fake. This is my reply to that interpretation. That uniform that is required while you are working probably wouldn't be as accepted if you were just hanging out. That tie and those heels probably would be uncomfortable at the gym. You dress differently for work. So behaving differently while you are there is not a far stretch. I call it putting on a personality uniform. Your uniform doesn't change the person wearing it. Likewise your personality uniform doesn't negate who you are, the fundamental you.

We will discuss strategic personality placement later. As for right now, as a Customer Server, you must understand that your boss saw something in you. The noticeable attributes of your personality was exactly what they were looking for to fill the position. Your boss has listened to the advice spoken by the business. The business explained in clear and precise words what type of Customer Server is necessary to represent the product, to facilitate the brand of CX that was created prior to your arrival. They are looking for no one else. So, knowing you were strategically chosen, pretending to be someone else throws a wrench in the strategy set in motion. Your disingenuousness makes you the weak link in the massive chain of CX that is crucial in the success of the business. You, then, taint the CX that the customers are expecting. The best Customer Server should have a personality that disengages any potential hostilities. We all have that 6th sense that can let us know when someone is being artificial. We can tell when someone is trying to pull the wool over our eyes. Our customers are no exclusion from that fact, making the Customer Server's interaction with the Customer crucial. A customer walks in your store. They encounter your Customer Server. Immediately the customer believes that the Customer Server is trying too hard; or, they believe the Customer Server is being disingenuously nice. You know what happens next: total and possible irreparable disconnection. The Grand Opportunity is tainted, making the customer's experience negative or at least uncomfortable, disabling you from being able to make the sale. How many stores have you walked out simply because you didn't like the Customer Server, the way they spoke, the way they laughed; some comment they made that just rubbed you the wrong way. That was your sixth sense kicking in warning you. The delicate synergy between the Customer Server and customer was doused out because of the Customer Servers fake personality. Encounters like that imbues lasting distaste for a product or service. How many times have you purchased something and months later the largest memory you have of that moment was how you were treated? Being really nice is great. But being REAL when being nice is better.

Be A Teacher

The best Customer Server is not just a sales person. He or she is so engaged that they magically transform in to an educator every time they clock-in. They were educated so well prior to being placed in front of the customers that their wealth of knowledge is massive. The training process was informative, precise, and fulfilling. They are now a high-powered rifle of information with a hair trigger. As a result, this wealth of knowledge and understanding has produced preparedness and confidence that is more than noticeable on the Customer Server's countenance, their demeanor, and in the words spoken. Confidence in the Customer Server produces confidence in the customer.

Going home totally confused or unaware how to use a product isn't fun. It produces, often times, regret. How many products have you purchased that is resting in the dark crevasses and recesses of your closet, storage room, or garage because you gave up trying to understand it? This should never happen. The Customer Server selling the product should have at least offered to show the customer how to use the item. "This can be a little intricate. Would you like for me to give you a demonstration?" You are asking a simple question, nothing intrusive – simply offering the "B side" of selling a product called HELP.

Your Customer Server cannot teach if they don't know. It should be mandatory to have not only a comprehensive training program for all of your existing and new hires, but also some type of continuing education must be implemented to keep your Customer Servers focused and honed. Reading industry materials: magazines, websites, blogs, should be part of their job description. Your Customer Servers should be totally au courant with all trends and highly perceptive about upcoming trends as well. If you need to prescribe to relevant periodicals and give them to your Customer Servers, conduct seminars and have an industry professionals to visit and deliver a speech about the product and commerce, pay to send your Customer Servers to training, whatever it takes do it.

The benefits are not only directed to the Customer Server, but also to you. According to the US Census Bureau 1998, 1999, 2000, a person with a college degree earns $1 million over his/her life time as compared to a person with only a high school diploma. A person with a college degree annual salary averages $52k; whereas, a person with only a high school diploma averages $30k a year. Now, I'm not touting college over OJT. I'm attempting to settle the position that knowledge produces wealth. I understand that you have a simple "Mom and Pop" ice cream parlor in downtown Sleepytown. And you don't see the ROI on educating your Customer Servers in the art of creamery. So, what does the comparison of degrees to diplomas have to do with you? Good question. Ask yourself why do degrees make more than diplomas? Two reason:

1. Degrees translate in to a heightened education. Employers believe those with degrees are smarter.

2. People with degrees are more educated thus producing confidence in their potential employer. Confidence allows the employer to feel comfortable about paying them a salary, that $52k as opposed to $30k. Education produces confidence.

Translate this into words that affect your business? Ok. Fully educated Customer Servers appear knowledgeable (educated) which in turn allows your customers to feel comfortable about letting you sell to them.

Once I was in a neighborhood coffee shop. I ordered a white mocha with a double pump of hazelnut syrup. The young lady making the drink looked at me with surprise. She walked over to the register where I stood waiting to pay for my drink. She said: "You must really like your drinks sweet." I said: "No, I actually don't like sweet coffee drinks." She responded: "Well your order will be sweeter than any coffee drink you can imagine." She said further: "I'll make it for you. Let you taste it. If you don't like it, I'll put less hazelnut in it for you or make it a regular mocha instead of a white mocha to offset the sweetness." She made the drink. And just like she said, my drink was as sweet as a spoon full of honey. Her education concerning coffee mixtures was very valuable. She would not have known the error in my order had she not be educated/trained properly.

Another example: the same coffee house, this time my wife. Annually my wife falls in to the full throws of orgasmic convulsions when coffee houses start selling pumpkin spice anything. This particular day, my wife orders her third mocha with a shot of pumpkin spice syrup. Because we frequented this coffee house, the young lady making the drink walked to us and asked: "Can I suggest something?" Now, messing with the wife's coffee drink is like poking a beehive with a stick. I guess because intrigue got the best of her that day she responded: "Yes?" The barista said: "I'm gonna put a shot of white mocha in your drink. Trust me. Tell me what you think." My wife looked at this lady like she was a frog in a new pond. But said, "ok" nevertheless. "If you don't like it. I'll throw it away and make the drink you ordered," the barista said. Long story short, my wife now buys white mocha mix from the coffee shop along with puréed pumpkin and makes the baristas suggested drink at home. The way she holds her coffee cup in the mornings, and sips her pumpkin spice white mocha is borderline infidelity, believe me. What can we learn from this? An educated Customer Sever will sell better than one that has no clue. That new drink of my wife's was $2 more than her normal one. And it produced ancillary revenue from my wife purchasing the coffee shops ridiculously expensive coffee syrups. Someone just hired to make coffee would not have known to make the suggestion. Education produced higher revenue.

There's an old African proverb: "Each one teach one." It should be incumbent on you to fully teach your Customer Server about your product. Their education will produce confident in them and in your customer, which will allow them to educate your customers.

Be Appreciative

Being an excellent Customer Server means going through numerous awkward situations. Often they are placed in moments that may make them feel uncomfortable. For example, in the hotel industry, the breakfast host is expected to spark conversations with total strangers eating their breakfast, still dazed by their sleep. Car dealers are asked to walk up to people who have developed a preconceived idea that they are con artists and these car salespeople are still expected to make a sale. Let's not forget those salespeople of the old regime, who still go door to door to sale their product. Believe it or not there are still people walking up to resident doors, walking up to businesses unannounced, totally undaunted by the seemingly impossible task of cold calling, not just cold calling, but cold calling on people, we've learned, that have PTPS (Post Traumatic Purchasing Syndrome) It is certainly fair to say that Customer Servers suffer many peculiar scenarios. What can make these types of scenario easier? If not easier, what can motivate Customer Servers or at least make the situation more tolerable? Appreciation. My mother has a saying: "If you can't be anything else, be thankful."

What is a simple way to define being thankful or appreciative?

1. Realizing that one's employment status could be starkly different. It could easily be nonexistent.

2. Realizing that one's boss could have just as easily chosen someone else.

3. Realizing that there are worse jobs.

So, taking these three facts in to consideration, one must accept (acceptance is key) or understand the affirmative vantage point and approach all duties in this light. It's simple right? We all are just seconds away from being the sun-burned, pathetic-looking, unfortunate person holding that "I'll work for food" cardboard sign at the intersection of Walmart and Family Dollar. How many of us were dangling on the cusp of financial destruction in the "Great Recession" of 2008? Me? I was newly unemployed when Fanny Mae and Freddy Mac collapsed. If I possessed the artistic abilities of the most talented and prolific artist, I could not paint an appropriate picture of the despair and hopelessness I felt looking for employment during that time. Jobs were so scarce that companies were told not to hand out applications – APPLICATIONS PEOPLE! Companies instructed their staff to deny other people pieces of paper. Jobs were so few that even applying for a job was prohibited. It was a nightmare. I went 3 months; daily, spending 8 hours every day looking for employment, simultaneously watching my savings account diminish like sands through the hour glass, watching my daughter eating unhealthy food because it was the cheapest, watching my wife pretend she wasn't hungry because she didn't want to partake in the slow devouring of our food supply. I remember it being so emotionally intense that my wife and I argued once about just how many slices of cold cuts I should use in a sandwich. It was horrible.

From that experience I've learned one of the most important life lessons: to be appreciative of my employment. My appreciation wasn't just another neurological pathway developed in my cerebral cortex. It wasn't just another notch scratched in the wall of my life. It was a personality change. Being unemployed during the greatest recession since the 1930's transformed my propensity, my bent toward being employed. I had a very interesting vantage point from whence to view my job now.

Eventually I found a job, one with significantly less pay than my previous one, with a demotion in position, and with profoundly younger coworkers. You know what? At that point, I could care less. Those things were about as important to me as rain is to fish in the ocean. I went from being an executive and making all the decisions to watching lesser astute executives making the wrong decisions. I mopped; I swept; I plunged toilets; I carried luggage—all happily. The words "above and beyond" are terms used too frequently. I went above and beyond and farther still.

Once I managed a hotel in a downtown area. An upscale hotel but the homeless frequented our lobby and lobby restroom as often as our paying guests. One afternoon a guest walked up to the front desk and informed the agents and bellman there was a "mess" in the restroom. One of our non-paying guests left a parting gift – certainly not a duty (no pun intended) for the squeamish. The bellman, without being prompted, jumped to the occasion and made matters better. Later, I pulled him to the side and asked why he volunteered. There were multiple people around that were responsible for public areas. He just laughed and said: "Man, I'm just thankful I got a job."

Appreciation will make any difficult situation tolerable. The best Customer Server appreciates the opportunity afforded them by the company. This appreciation is displayed in their quick response, their enthusiasm, in their actions toward the task and the customer. There were, I'm sure, other applicants. If not, I'm sure also, their CAN be other applicants. All your Customer Servers should reward you with appreciation by representing the company, the product; the service offered with their best- their best everything.

Here are some signs of a Customer Server that appreciates their position;

1. **Attire**: even if they are wearing a uniform, a clean, ironed uniform is a sign that they are

concerned about themselves and about how they are being seen by the customer.

2. **Efficiency**: the extent to which they perform and complete required duties indicate that they are not just a present, warm body but someone actually there to make his superiors and customers happy.

3. **Attitude:**
   a. *Attitude* both when praises and criticism is given. The ability to navigate both really shows sincerity and willingness to adapt and grow.
   b. *Attitude* when customers are treating them nicely and when they are being mistreated. Gold is purified in fire. The true Customer Server comes in to the light in high and intense emotional situations.
   c. *Attitude* toward their teammates. A true Customer Server's main concern is the success of your product or service and the happiness and satisfaction of your customers, not the intensity or the importance of their friendship of their teammates. A true customer server is not concerned that they are not the best of friends with their coworkers.
   d. *Attitude* away from work. An appreciative Customer Server speaks very fondly of their place of employment.

4. **Willingness:** An appreciative Customer Server will do almost doing anything within reason. They are not push overs; but, people that have experienced the "dark side of the moon" and are aware that doing something that isn't exactly what you want

to do is incredibly better than not being able to do anything at all.

5. **Participation:** Although the appreciative Customer Server is extremely willing and gung-ho, they are not just fetchers. They are involved. One of the best Customer Server is ones that respectfully challenges decisions and gives input.

6. **Confidence:** This confidence can appear to be arrogance to an untrained eye, especially to the eyes of a coworker with lesser interest in their own success, much less yours or your product or service. This confidence is translated in to product knowledge, which fosters a confidence in the Customer Server and confidence in your product or service from the customer.

It's really rare to find all of the above 6 attributes in on Customer Server. However, please look for them and know that the individual with 3 or more is a keeper! They are the Customer Server you've been looking for. Sink your hooks in them and, by hook or crook, never let them go.

Ways To Lose Customers

Underestimate The Importance of Communication:

Often when I speak to owners and department heads, I'm often given a weird look when I talk about the following topic. This is because, #1, I'm passionate about this subject. #2, this subject is a topic not often broached by customer service experts.

Imagine this scenario: a customer experiences a horrible incident with a product. This experience causes the customer to become very angry. This customer, now, mired in their unhappiness calls the company's customer service center to obtain aid in this matter. The call is made; the customer is tossed around like a hot potato, only to finally speak to someone that has more difficulty speaking English than an infant.

How dare you as an owner of a business, how dare you as an influence in the hiring process have such disdain, such a diminished concern about my experience and my concerns that you don't bother hiring people that are able to communicate. Really? Am I so low on the totem of your daily business transactions that hiring articulate, friendly, intelligent, enthusiastic sounding people to answer your phone is beyond you? I'm not just referring to non-English speaking individuals. I'm encompassing people who plainly just sound like nincompoops on the phone. You know, those people who have more "aaaah's, and eeerrr's" in a sentence than a pirate. It's just not cool.

Here are two super important "games" you are losing by not hiring knowledgeable, articulate Customer Servers:

- **<u>The Game of Customer Appreciation</u>:** Your customer had choices. They chose you. In that customer you have something that your competitor doesn't have: that particular customer. In business there are many games played. You win every time a customer calls your business, every time a customer hires you. Earlier, I defined Customer Service as a grand opportunity. It is a grand opportunity for you to show how appreciative you are that you were chosen out of many. Professional sales people have created an industry on how to sell a product. There are books, and CD's, and DVD's, all to instruct us on how to sell our product. It's my opinion (and believe me, I'm no master salesperson) that on the checklist of making a sale, demonstrating appreciation should be task number one. Demonstrating appreciation, firstly, by actually saying how appreciative you are. Then, and equally important if you ask me, show your appreciation by placing the right person in front of your customers. Your Customer Server's readiness, product intelligence, enthusiasm, and willingness to serve tell your customer how thankful you are they chose you. Your Customer Server is like a champion, an advocate charged with the holistic protection of their experience and their purchase. Not only that, the quality of said advocate or champion speaks to the extent to which you hold their experience and purchase valuable. There's nothing you can say to convince me that you hold my experience and purchase in high regard if the person hired to protect them can't understand the words coming out of my mouth. In the whole scheme of readiness, our customers are very longsuffering. They understand that product intelligence is a process. Learning a product fully takes time. Because our customers understand this, they will allow some semblance of ignorance. "I understand you are new or you're not sure; but, is there someone available that can answer my questions?" That would be our customer's tolerant and patient response to lack of product intelligence. However, and this is a pretty significant "however", there are some attributes that our customers just assume are self-evident and ubiquitous. That is the ability to speak and understand the current national language, the ability to communicate to them additional information concerning their potential purchase. "Are you kidding me? This is the advocate and champion over my purchase and experience, someone who can't pronounce the words champion or experience – someone that makes Mongo in the movie Blazing Saddle seem like a radio personality?" That is what I imagine our customer asking themselves when they call your phone bank, or walk in to your hardware store and find your non-communicative Customer Server.

Hold your customer in higher regard. Hold their experience in higher regard. Place the best person you can in front of them. Your Customer server is like a Halmark card with feet, a head, and a butt. Give them a heart-felt Halmark card by expressing you sentiment with best Customer Server you can find.

- **<u>The Game Of Product Representation</u>**: You have loss this game horribly when you hire people that can barely speak English. Again, earlier we discussed that the

Customer Sever represents you. They represent your product. They represent the message you are trying to get across to the community. Most of all, it is their primary job to be able to articulate your vision, to verbally paint an enticing picture that would sway your customer to patronize you. Hiring people that cannot communicate effectively is like hiring someone who is legally blind to paint a family portrait. If I hire a blind person to paint a portrait of my family, there no way that the artist, although well-intentioned I'm sure, can capture the strikingly rugged yet adorable features I possess. It's impossible. The artist's physical limitations make it so. Likewise is the outcome of hiring a Customer Server than can't speak well. They are painting a distorted picture of you, your business, and what you are selling.

Product representation harkens back to when we discussed Post Traumatic Purchasing Disorder. Our customers are expecting you to overcharge them; they are expecting you to be pushy. This is their expectation walking in to your doors. Placing the right person to be the personification of your product or service eases all misgivings. Our customers are comforted and encouraged and find validation in their purchase from the Customer Server. How much comfort are you getting when you are spending more time playing the "What?" game with some stranger on the phone? There's no comfort accomplished in all honesty. Intense frustration is accomplished and that customer walks away with a very bad taste in their mouth about your product.

Communication is the key to gaining, maintaining, and losing your customers.

Belittle Them

I met a guy that owned a gas station years ago. He owned a gas station on the *"wrong side of the tracks."* Like most convenience stores, he sold more than gas. His patrons bought as much alcoholic beverages as they did gas.

Beneficial to the owner, his gas station's competition was a couple miles away. He was the only store in the neighborhood. He was always extremely busy. Unfortunately, though, this owner felt he didn't need to be friendly, partly because his patrons had no other choice, mostly because his patrons were at the lower end of the income spectrum. I witnessed many situations where the owner displayed his frustration either because someone bothered him while he was doing paper work, or simply because the customer didn't purchase enough in his opinion. He would yell; he would huff and puff; he would roll his eyes; he would toss the customer's change at them.

A few years later another gas station opened directly across the street. Guess what? Those frustrating low income customers starting patronizing the second store and the other was boarded up and closed within a year and a half. They literally stopped shopping at his store-- completely.

How much of a nut-job are you for being a willing participant in the service industry but yet easily frustrated by serving? How ridiculous does the following scenario sound? You are a team member of a business that relies heavily on customers calling; but, you hate your job because the phone rings a lot. You are a team member of a business that sell products that are very intricate (computers, stock, etc) and you find yourself angry every day because people are asking too many questions. You are a manager of a business that is open 24 hours, and you are frustrated because you get phone calls in the wee hours of the morning. And finally, you are a team member of a business that obtains most of their business or clientele on Friday through Sunday, and you complain that you rarely get a weekend off. If you ask me, the above scenarios represent the definition of stupidity. Those types of Customer Servers should not only be terminated, but instructed to never work in the industry as long as the industry exists. These types of Customer Servers spend their whole shift being angry and annoyed. Further, they exact their anger and frustrations on their patrons. Their tone of voice, their facial expression, and their sarcastic comments are all attempts to belittle your customers because they are profoundly unhappy people.

We visited an Italian restaurant in upstate New York. While there we unintentionally embittered our server. You see, my daughter was deeply shy. She would not speak to any adults with the exception of her parents and her teachers. For

10 years my wife and I ordered her food for her. We decided this day was the day she would order her own food. Well, when the server approached us for our order, my daughter was not ready. We requested to be allowed a few more minutes to get our order together. The waitress was extremely nice. She politely mentioned she would return shortly. When she did, our little one was still not ready, crying with fear, really not wanting to make her order. We asked, once again that we be given a few more minutes. The waitress' face lit up with a surprised look. She laughed and said: "Yeah, ok, because I got all day!" I wanted to explain to her we weren't intentionally making her day difficult. I wanted to explain how difficult it was for my child to speak to her. She made me, a paying customer, feel I needed to explain. I felt I had wrong her. Not exactly the right disposition to have as a customer. When in all actuality, she was wrong. As a Customer Server we must be ready and equipped for most scenarios to occur. Our waitress should have been aware that maybe, every now and then, customers may take an extended amount of time to decide on what they want to eat. She should have been prepared. She was not. Because she was not, she placed her unpreparedness on our shoulders. Sufficed to say, her actions were not amongst the most prudent ones. That particular restaurant was very close to a hotel that I managed. I removed all the menus for the restaurant out of my hotel. I informed my team of what happened. We NEVER suggested that restaurant again, at least while I was there.

I don't care how cataclysmic or arduous your day and night may be, if in the midst of the cataclysm and arduousness you cannot perform genuine, mind-blowing customer service you should not be allowed to assist any customer. Don't clock-in. Don't go to work. I've gotten in to numerous of heated discussions about that statement. Apparently there are a gaggle of people that believe despite your current disposition you should be allowed to aid customers. It's not a secret. There are peripheral stimuli that influence our frame of mind. There are countless days that I walk with tightly clinched butt cheeks because I want to choke innocent bystanders simply because my wife made me angry. It's not fair to the customers that we take out our frustrations on them. Whatever muscle you need to develop in your body, in your mind, in your inner self to enable you to separate your ill-feelings and your customer serving duties you need to do it.

Department heads, owners this topic needs be a no-brainer and deal-breaker for you. Ill treatment of your customers for any reason, bar none, should be the express route to unemployment. Your Customer Server, all of them, should be able to work through adversities, sickness, and pain, whatever. If they can't they should not be allowed in your Sterile Zone. We discussed this earlier, people!

Remember, your customers have a choice. THEY CHOSE YOU! Reward them with a demonstration of your appreciation. Despite the day you are having, make them feel you are ecstatic about their choice. ***Be honored by every customer.***

Make A Difficult Situation Technical

Our customers, very frequently, are visiting us because there's some type of problem, or some question that needs to be answered. Of course, there are instances when customers are purchasing simply because of leisure or pleasure. In today's economy, however, our customers are parting with their hard-earned money only if they have to.

Imagine this scenario: A customer suddenly has to purchase something (something broke, became missing, whatever). This customer, now, has to part with their finances and make unforeseen, unbudgeted purchases. This not-so-happy customer walks in to your shop, calls your business, logs in to your website and meets R2D2: Really Really Technical Dude Deluxe. R2D2 starts pilling off esoteric, industry vocabulary that makes you feel dumb as a wet dinner napkin. With every word spoken, you are tossing your head from one side to the other like a confused puppy. Your words say you understand; but, in your mind you're doing the most spot-on impression of Arnold on Different Strokes: "What chutalkin bout Willis?"

Everybody likes simple. Unless you are Alex Trebeck or a member of the Starship Enterprise you just want "the facts ma'am" Displaying the height, width, and breadth of your product vocab doesn't help a sale. Break it down. Don't get me wrong, many customers will understand every technical word that falls off your lips. They get it totally, talk about hard drives, bandwidth, and data management. But, more times than not, you get those customers who just want the computer they saw on the commercial. Some customers just want their car to crank. It is these customers that you have to be very careful that you do not bludgeon them unconscious with complicated information.

In my experience, hotel phone repair guys are notorious for that. These guys would walk through my hotel doors wearing cargo shorts or worn jeans, dangling all types of telephony repairing gadgets off their belts, wearing boots with the steel toe exposed. Shortly after saying hello and perusing the telephone equipment, they would commence to spewing (for me anyway) unintelligible, multi-syllable descriptions of my equipment faultiness. One time I actually stopped a guy mid-sentence and said: "Man, get outta here. You're making those words up. There's no such thing as an Incumbent Multi-exchange Center." They would always make me feel lost as a computer salesman in an Amish town. I literally dreaded calling them

Remember, you are the guardian of your customer's experience and purchase. Their experience depends largely on how they feel and how you make them feel. They are already feeling angry, said, disappointed. Don't make them feel like an elementary student in a geothermal magno-electric nuclear ion lecture. Survey the customer. Tacitly test the extent to their knowledge of the product. If their knowledge falls just short of "say what?" then make your pitch, your sale as Sesame Street as possible without insulting the customer. Remember (1) Knowledge is power. The more the customer knows, the more empowered they are. (2) Cx doesn't end once the customer has the receipt and walks to their vehicle. It extends throughout the life of the product or service. If that customer can return home and feel good about their purchase, then the purchase was a good one and the customer services was successful. At the same token, if the customer returns home confused, unsure, or totally lost about their purchase, you have failed as a Customer Server. Make the customer understand. Understanding breeds Comfortability and Comfortability loosens the white-knuckled grip off the wallet.

Chapter 4

Milking Your Cows

Human beings are enigmatic on a cellular level. We are the only beings on earth that are able to smile, to hug someone, to dance wildly at a party, and at the same time be angry with our spouse or have a migraine. Outwardly we bear a smile with brightness that rivals the sun; but, inwardly we harbor resentment that would frighten someone if they were aware. Mixed signals are a talent for humans. "Objects in the mirror may be closer than they appear."

Not only are the signals we give off mixed, but sometimes those signals are just plain weird- not weird as in an "ALF" sense of the term but weird because of unfamiliarity. Upbringings, backgrounds, beliefs, experiences as a child and as an adult all are components to how we carry ourselves. They are major influences on how we interact with others. They influence how we pursue our goals, how we prioritize, and how we mold our morals and values.

Now take in consideration the myriad of building blocks that construct a person's personality and the millions of different ways those building blocks have been influenced in their construction. Imagine those building blocks in a team of people looking, seeking your expertise, waiting for instruction for their success, and the ability to feed themselves and their families. Dozens, sometimes hundreds of different attitudes, personalities are surrounding you—sometimes making things difficult—all of which are your responsibility. Their development, their understanding are all weighted upon your shoulders. I think it's fair to say that owners, managers, supervisors, and team leads have a heaping pile of things on their plates.

As a department head these invisible variables make our mission difficult to achieve. Daily we walk in to a building filled with land mines, personalities that could blow up in your face or they could create an explosive moment of creativity. We never know. This is why, while we are groping through the dark desperately seeking something we can consider "DEFINITE," something that will allow us to breathe a sigh of relief, we should hold close to our bosoms all the jewels, all the precious accomplishments we achieve as it relates to managing people. Once in a while we obtain a tool that makes it easier to be leaders, easier to squeeze out of the people we manage success and an accomplished mission, tools that help us navigate the choppy waters that is being a manager.

If you are a manager like me, you like affording EVERYONE the benefit of the doubt. You see potential in all of your coworkers. You hold everyone to the same level of expectation. You are like a parent not wanting to display any favoritism to any particular child, placing all of your team members on the one small pedestal, pushing them all in to one cramped area. When one team member seems to be failing, you like a loving mother eagle, will swoop down and catch them and place the fallen eaglet back on the crowded pedestal.

That kind of action works perfectly in the realm of parenting and being an eagle, not so much as it relates to being a leader. One of the most difficult lessons for me to learn was that all my team members are NOT created equally. Our team members are not like the Borg, the emotionless, tunnel-vision automaton race of people on "Star Trek The Next Generation." The Borg were all interconnected, each one – though there were many- possessed one thought, one voice. It was all about "the collective" not the individual. I had to learn that I was working with INDIVIDUALS; and, the individual possessed strengths and weaknesses. Unfortunately for me, those strengths proved to be beneficial and hindrances.

That was, seriously, a difficult nut to crack for me. If there was an open position, I would fill the position with the best person out of the litany that applied. I would schedule people to work base upon who was willing to work. Cooperation and loyalty were important traits for me back then. I would reprimand them on non-specific infractions like "not smiling" or "not sounding happy" or "not being polite." Then at the end of each month I would look at my customer service scores and be amazed that I didn't achieve my goal. I would fall in to my monthly distraught mode, panicking, and wondering why and where did I fail.

I eventually learned to Milk My COWS, which essentially means to gather around me a Coalition Of the Willing. I learned not just to gather them but to utilized or "milk" them as best as I can. Here are erroneous thoughts we have as leaders:

1. Everyone has the same goal. Sure, most want their place of employment to be successful. Success in the place of employment translates in to job stability and longevity and a constant paycheck. That doesn't mean that every team member is willing to do what it takes to make their place of employment successful.

2. Everyone has the same motive. I promise you, a person looking for a career is a markedly different team member compared to a person who obtained the position simply because there was a position available. A person who depends on their position to feed themselves and several children is a different employee compared to a student in college on a full scholarship that is, for the most part, working for beer and mall money.

3. A hard worker or person that works a lot of hours isn't the best person for the job. Never confuse the number of hours worked for quality of hours worked. Dedication does not always mean best.

The plight of a leader is often a silent torture. Nobody knows the trouble we see. Everyone has the luxury of minimal responsibility. Our responsibilities span in to areas that most team members are not aware:

a Staff development

b Financial and revenue goals

c Physical maintenance

d Customer relations and retention

e Product development and the list go

on and on.

Two of the most difficult tasks that come along with being a leader are seeking help for team members and accepting help from our team members. As a leader you should actively seek help from people in your circle. Leaders are pros at multi-tasking; but, we are far from being octopi. Leaders are "heavy lifters." Focus on the tasks that are significantly consequential to you as a department head. The rest can be divvyed out to our support team.

For years as a hotel manager my Mondays were replete with reports that recap the prior week. These reports would literally consume my entire day. I would start them at 7am and finish around 5pm. Some were small reports requesting information that was easily obtainable. The rest were highly intensive, incredibly sensitive reports that requested information that required research and detailed explanation. I performed those reports for approximately 8 years before I allowed myself to delegate the less sensitive ones. Once I did, my Mondays were not the weekly horror that I experienced for many years. I didn't know what to do with myself. So much stress was removed and I, for the first time in many years I did not dread to go to sleep on Sundays. Once I experienced the most refreshing sigh of relief since the existence of inhaling. I began fervently looking for other tasks to hand out. The more I had off my plate, the more I could focus with a clear mind on the "heavy lifting." My hotel ran better. I eliminated considerably the number of overlooked and forgotten issues that my boss would frequently notice his visits. I became a sharper manager, a more intoned leader.

Accepting Help From Others

I guess prior to arriving at my epiphany about delegating, I enjoyed saying: "I don't have time," or "Not right now, I have too much to do." It made me feel important. My desk was totally covered with paper. My computer displayed excels charts that resembled highly classified documents. My pen was stuck behind my ears. My calculator was clicking as if it was sending Morse code. All of this aided in the appearance of high responsibility. This went on for years until one particular hotel that was literally suffering from my absence, from me being constantly distracted. I lamented to a team member: "If I could just get help. I could focus more on what is actually damaging our hotel." And, the team member responded. "I ask you every day is there anything I can do to help?" Sometimes the answer to our questions is as obvious as the nose on our face. I had an experienced co-worker actively seeking to help remove the monkey off of my back. I was equally as active denying them the chance.

Once I did, my life became soo much more enjoyable.

In my experience, I've encountered 4 types of co-workers. I will explain their benefit and hindrances.

1. **The Career Builder**

      a. Pro: These team members are pursuing opportunities to sustain their lives in the industry. These people are highly interested, personally involved, and constantly looking to learn more.

      b. Con: Their loyalty is not so much to the leader, but to capturing the opportunity for advancement. They are often know-it-alls as they have most likely worked numerous other locations making them intransigent and unwilling to change.

2. **The Loyal Follower**: This person finds great satisfaction in pleasing the leader. They find great worth in being led. They will perform wonderfully just to make management happy.

a. Pro: They are extremely dependable, trustworthy, and open to instructions

b. Con: The have very little ambition. Original thought is not something they possess. Their ability to perform at a high level is replaced solely with making sure the boss isn't mad.

3. **The Shooting Star**: This person only seeks to be helpful for a short time. These are your college students, teachers in the summer, former execs looking to sustain themselves until they find another executive position.

a. Pro: The people are timely because tuition, bills, responsibilities are their main concern.

b. Their loyalty is to themselves and their short term goal. Their interests are very minimal.

4. **The Incumbent Worker:** These people are working solely to sustain their lives: to buy gas for their vehicle, to buy groceries for

themselves and/ or their families, to pay rent. Maintaining a stable life is their fuel to life

    a.   Pro: Extremely dependable, flexible, would work many shifts and cross train if necessary, very open to instructions

    b.   Con: Often desperate, very high stressed, loyalty is not to the department head but more so to the fear of going without.

There are many more I'm sure. However, these are the type of team members I've encountered. It is your responsibility to determine which type is working with you. I find that determining what type of team members I have around me is vital. Don't be afraid to literally ask your team members their goals, their expectations of the company and of themselves both personally and professionally. These might be the type of questions or types of answers you seek in the interview process.

Remember you have a desire, need, expectation for success. You have people that have the same expectation of you. Use as many tools that you have at your disposal. Once you've made these determinations, gather or create a coalition of the willing. Together embark upon a journey for success for you and your COWs.

Chapter 5

Strategic Hiring

N work with the public. One thing that makes my teeth itch is a person that call themselves a "people person." I've done hundreds of interviews in my life time, at various corners of this great country of ours. I've found that it is inevitable to have someone tell me that they are a "people person." What exactly does being a "people person" mean? After more probing, I have often found that the self-proclaimed "people person" had rarely been outside of their state. Really? You've found this confidence in your ability to interact with the public, so much so that you've dubbed yourself a "people person" and you haven't even spoken to someone outside of your own circle? Do people cease to exist beyond your own state line? Most often it would be those "people persons" that would crumble under pressure during any altercation with a customer. I would ask myself: "Why is that people person weeping uncontrollably because a customer spoke to them in a "not nice" tone?" "Why is that people person yelling at that customer?" If anyone ever speaks the words "I'm a people person," look them directly in the pupils and say, "Sure, whatever."

As we have learned in previous chapters, personalities can be numerous as the stars in the sky. Also the influences on those personalities can be just as numerous. Personalities are like an enigma rapped in a labyrinth, wrapped in a puzzle, and then placed in the pitch black darkness. They are delicate entities also. Although I am a believer that personalities can never be completely understood, it is in my opinion possible to detect patterns in certain personalities. For instances, I've noticed that people who overwhelmingly display a happy demeanor have certain capabilities and short comings. Further, those who maintain a dead-panned, robotic professional demeanor have a totally different set of capabilities and short comings.

The American Psychological Associations says personalities "refers to individual differences in characteristic patterns of thinking, feeling and behaving.….understanding individual difference in particular personality characteristics, such as sociability or irritability".

There's something driving us, controlling us to make the decisions we make, to have the preferences we have, to have the abilities we have. All of the important characteristics are influenced by our personalities. Having an understanding of the drivers would certainly help us understand our team members better. More importantly, if used correctly, an acumen on personalities could help us strategically place our team members, especially new hires, in areas that allow them to be successful. A person with what we deem a "good personality" isn't necessary the best person to man the phones. A 'good personality" doesn't always translate over the phone. Or, someone extremely happy and ebullient may not be the person you want unloading a supply truck. Their personality could be beneficial elsewhere. Strategic personality placement is a new concept in most service-oriented businesses. Those involved with hiring either don't bother to know or are not aware of the importance of personalities and how they translate to our customers.

I don't in anyway profess to be a scientist, a philosopher, or a sociologist. I don't possess any educational accolades that speak to my acute acumen and proficiency to human personalities. All I have are the tools that have aided me, the tools that have afforded me success. Other people, professional or otherwise, can dispute the validity. What are irrefutable are my successes. There are countless hotels with heightened customer service scores because I chose to strategically hire and place particular personalities in areas where I felt best suited them.

My research has turned up many personality types. Philosophers, both past and present, believe there are 3 basic personality types. I've found scientist that believe there are 6 core personality types, all given different names. Some of the names sound extremely similar to other expert's names. My experience has uncovered 3 personality types that I feel are overwhelmingly in the service-based industry. We'll delve in to these personalities and discuss their pros and cons. Also, we will discuss what type of task or job is best fit for the personality.

The Methodical

My experiences with this personality type has taught me that The Methodical can be either the most efficient customer service professional or a complete train wreck. Depending on the type of business, the market of your business, and the type of clientele, the characteristics of The Methodical will fit perfectly or be a square peg in round hole.

All behaviors, habits, and predilections are conditioned, meaning after numerous attempts or trials of a behavior and their positive or negative outcome, the behavior has either conditioned (taught) us to continue the behavior, to do them less frequently, or to never try that behavior again. Positive outcome of a behavior are called rewards and the negative ones are often named consequences. Based upon the size of the reward or consequence (or our perception of the size) we will hold firmly to these behaviors and attach them to our being (our personality) or do all that is physically possible to stay away from those behaviors (fear/phobia).

Life has conditioned The Methodical to prefer the "method" of an act. They perceive great worth with having or process extreme fear of being without the method. As a result, the characteristics of The Methodical are prudence. In this instance don't misconstrue prudence with having a heightened intellect. Prudence in a Methodical personality means being cautious, precise usage of discretion, not reckless. The Methodical has developed a strong distaste for mistakes. So if a course of action requires The Methodical to go through A and B to get to C, The Methodical will spend a lot of time navigating the A portion of the action before they attempt to expending an incredible amount of time with action B, in order to, assuredly, accomplish action C. The Methodical is willing to sacrifice speed and time to achieve accomplishment. The end doesn't justify the means. The end is the means.

The strong affinity for prudence has created an equally strong affinity for analyzing. The Methodical will analyze all situations before moving forward. Analyzing affords them information regarding potential dangers, mistakes, and the like. Their need to analyze can also be considered due diligence. After intense due diligence The Methodical acquires the level of comfort to proceed. After the receipt of definite assurance that the expected outcome will occur, The Methodical will make the decision, proceed with the task, and finish the request. This isn't by any means an indication of fear. The Methodical has placed quality very high on their priority list. Their pursuit for high quality has made them cautious, unwilling to move forward with being properly abreast, properly prepared.

The result to all the prudence and analyzing is most often order. Order or systemization is the cherry on top for this type of personality. Everything has its own place, not just a place but its own proper place, a place where it is most effective and efficient. The Methodical has learned that proper utilization, correct placement will make any task easier and likely faster in the long run. Also, the result will produce a better quality of product.

What is most attractive about The Methodical is their intense desire to do the right thing. Often The Methodical is very moralistic and profoundly trustworthy. Their trustworthiness stems from their constant production of positive outcomes. Any assigned task will be fulfilled and all expected outcomes will be accomplished. This is very beneficial to The Methodical's place of employment; but, to this personality type positive outcomes are a must. The route taken to reach the outcome must be the same; the positioning of all tools and aids must be the same in order to obtain the expected outcome. If the expected outcome is not achieved, then there is disorder. Something was not in the proper place. Realizing that The Methodical depends on cautiousness and proper utilization they can be trusted to perform.

The Methodical really takes time to learn the A portion of the equation before they attempt to make the attempt to take on the B portion. It is this pain-staking slow delivery, getting to know all angles of a task that gives The Methodical a heightened sense of judgment. This personality type has not learned their job but has lived and made the learning process a memorable experience, an experience that is readily recalled at any given moment. The Methodical's ability to regurgitate information makes them the most professional at making decisions in their assigned task. For a lot of personalities, when it is decision making time, it's really just a roll of the dice, a game of chance and hopes. The Methodical knows, he's living experience and will be the best person to contact when something is wrong. The Methodical's advice comes from living all angles of the process and profound knowledge. The Methodical's decisions are sound and often the most logical.

The Impassioned

The second personality type could easily be considered the opposite end of the spectrum compared to The Methodical. If the Methodical is Robin, then The Impassioned is most certainly Batman. The Impassioned will ultimately be the representation, the person out front as the face of your product or service.

Being in the forefront of your business will turn out to be the perfect place for The Impassioned. The Impassioned's greatest attribute is their emotional involvement. Your business is much more to this personality type than somewhere to go for a few hours, much more than a salary or paycheck. The Impassioned becomes personally involved. The Methodical will find worth in a job. The Impassioned attaches their responsibilities to themselves. It becomes their lives. It becomes their identity. That is more than appreciation and empathy. It is fervent, passionate, desirousness to get the job done. Simply put, The Impassioned believes whole-heartedly in you and your product.

A person that is personally invested is the right person for the job as a representative for your company.

The personal involvement will raise the intensity in which The Impassioned will sell you service. The failure of your business is considered a life failure, similar to a person being held underwater to drown. The impassioned will fight violently to breathe again. They will do what it takes to be successful. This intensity can be found in hours worked. Working long hours is no problem and honestly much preferred. Calls after hours are not only no problem, but often met with enthusiasm. Their work ethic is impeccable. The Impassioned ambition is practically sewn in every garment they wear. They possess a strong desire to achieve and reach high levels. They are dreamers, seeing the present as a catalyst to grander opportunities. In their minds, they've mapped out the journey and all that is necessary to gain success. Obstacles are mere hindrances and always surmountable.

Don't mistake The Impassioned as unrealistic dreamers. They are fully aware of the future short comings and failures. They don't care. Their personal involvement and white-heated ambitions fuel them, strengthens them, motivates them, and in the eyes of The Impassioned they are capable of weathering any storm to achieve their goal.

This ambition produces lots of ideas and possible solutions. Don't be surprised if The

Impassioned isn't somewhat off putting by their non-stop discussion of their dreams, slightly incessant sharing of ideas. They are not unstable, flighty people; but, wholly engaged, ambitious go-getters.

The Impassioned is far from your fair weather friend also. Once again because they have invested so much of themselves in to the activity, the Impassioned are not easily swayed from their loyalties. They are supportive no matter the situation or circumstance. Good weather or bad, The Impassioned will choose to be loyal.

The flipside to The Impassioned ironically is often found in his passion. The Impassioned often tends to set unobtainable goals. They are visionary, heavy lifters. They also bite off more than they can chew. It is important to monitor your Impassioned team member. Monitor them with the knowledge that The Impassioned is viewing life, viewing the task at hand through glasses stained with their life blood. I cannot repeat enough how personally involved this personality type is with your product or service. Ever heard of the term "Blood Brother?" The Impassioned is yours. Because this is so, they tend to stretch themselves too far to reach the goal. Make sure your Impassioned is being realistic. In a restaurant scenario, you Impassioned will work many double shifts, as much as you are willing to assign. However, the human side of The Impassioned never fails to appear in the form of fatigue. Though dependability is a commodity, customer service issued with a side of tiredness is a deadly cocktail for failure. As a department head, you must bridle The Impassioned's passion. Gage it. Strategically use it when necessary. Also shelve it to be used at the correct moment.

The Congenial

Lastly and certainly not least, you have The Congenial. If The Methodical is Batman; and, The Impassioned is Robin. The Congenial is definitely Alfred The Butler. What separate all three definitely are the motives they possess in performing their duties. The Methodical is motivated by the task itself and its intricacies. The Impassioned is motivated by the outcome, success, the end. While The Congenial finds their motivation in your customers. The Congenial is the true Customer Server at heart. This personality type is a true servant.

I cringe and hesitate to use the word servant. It unfortunately carries with it an indelible negative connotation. Words like slave, mindless, ignorant comes to mind when we think of this word. Those words cannot be farther from the truth. Being a servant isn't an awful badge of dishonor to wear or position to hold. The servant is the person with an excellent workable acumen of what it takes to fulfill the needs of the customer, which is, by the way, job 1. The Congenial embodies the role of a true servant 100% despite the negative connotation.

One of the most attractive characteristic of the Congenial would be selflessness. The Congenial will have several thoughts in a day and most of them will be about someone else, not themselves. This personality will go the extra mile to ensure the pleasure of the customer even if it places them in an awkward position, even if it's uncomfortable and embarrassing. The Congenial is able to weather embarrassment and discomfort for the betterment of the customer. He/she will sacrifice their disposition to ensure the customer is satisfied.

The Congenial romantically sees pleasing the customer as enhancing the customer's lives, making them better people. It is this altruistic approach to customer service that makes them ideal. The Congenial has captured the notion that while the customer is in front of them, it is an opportunity to create something incredible. The Congenial working in a phone bank doesn't view the few moments, seconds, and minutes with the customer on the phone as a moment to divulge the scripted verbiage. They view it as an integral chance to produce level change in the person on the other end of the phone. If once the conversation is over and The Congenial has not caused a significant increase in your emotions, your temperament, your outlook, they experience extreme feelings of failure. The moment while the customer and The Congenial are together is inordinately consequential. They must inspire you. The must affect your life positively in some way.

As a department head this innate tendency to serve will prove beneficial. While some customers would find your Methodical too serious, others may consider your Impassioned uncomfortably enthused. You will definitely find that your customers are drawn to your Congenial because of their pleasing nature. They are far from being argumentative or conformational. While the other personality types have reasons to be protective: The Methodical will be offended if rushed, protecting the method. The Impassioned is totally driven by success, always protecting or fighting failure. The Congenial's main concern is the foundation of your business: the customer and their well-being. It can be demonstrated by an analogy about a fire fighting troop. While the members of the troop are charged with extinguishing the fire, some are assigned particular roles to achieve this end. Someone is responsible for transportation. Someone must be on hose duty. There's that one fire fighter who has been assigned to aim the water toward the fire. This action, while equally important as the others, affects the fire more than the others. The doused fire is caused by the aimed water more than any involvement. The Congenial is your aimed water because they are laser-focused on the customer. They tend to more pleasing, will to be cooperative, less combative in the eyes of the customer.

I think it would be an understatement to mention how pertinent it is for your customers to feel comfortable. Most customers, at the very core of them, have a deep-seated distrust for sales people. Remember Post Traumatic Purchasing Syndrome? Any car salesperson can attest to this point. Before they walk through your door, before they dial your number, the customer has settled in their mind that your sales person is going to upsell them. Often being behind the scenes we forget or underestimate how intelligent our customers are. With the now ubiquitous internet our patrons are learned people. If they are not learned, they have the instantaneous ability to find facts and the information at the touch of a button- of their cell phone no less- real data in real time in seconds. They know the price on the tag has been marked up, and sometimes they are aware of the percentage of the mark-up. They are armed with technology equipped with data. They know the game.

It is this knowledge that our customers have acquired that breeds a sense of distrust. An emotional bastion is automatically erected just before any interaction with the customer. Have you ever walked up to a customer and asked if you could be of any assistance, and that customer verbally snaps your head off like a junk yard dog protecting a bowl of kibble? This is because the customer has pulled the emotional and mental partition down to protect themselves from what they believe is your intentions to behave unscrupulously toward them. I worked in an outlet store in college. I can remember many-a-day where smiling happy-go-luck customers would immediately lose their smile because they saw me, someone with a tie and a name badge. Many customers created perfect 90 degree angles in their change of direction to escape my PERCIEVED evil claws. The service-oriented companies have taught the customers this behavior. Customers are displaying learned behavior. Customers Servers are dishonest; they are concerned only about making the sale, the commission, the bottom line.

You need someone that will softly disarm your customers, invite them to relax—someone that is the antithesis of what the customer is expecting or has wrongly imagined. Enter your Congenial.

You must be careful, however. The Congenial can often be an emotional time bomb. The Congenial will be the one that will develop relationships in the work place, relationships with their customers, and relationships with their teammates. It is not unusual for The Congenial to b so heavily involved with those around them that they would easily consider your customers family, especially the frequently returning customers. The Congenial will be the one that will be invited to personal gatherings. You would find multiple phone numbers of your customers as contacts in The Congenial phone. The Congenial will remember birthdays, holiday gifts, and special occasions. They are emotionally pinioned to your patrons.

The Congenial can be dangerous because of two reasons:

1. The emotional attachment can result in dishonesty, like giving discounts to friends—aka "hook-ups." The Congenial often places the relationship above their employment. In doing so, for instance, when you are not there the Congenial is heaping 3 scoops of ice cream on a waffle cone when they should be placing 1 on a regular cone. Further, some customers are predators. They can sense The Congenial's need for emotional attachment and prey upon it, obtaining perks of a feigned relationship.

2. The Congenial are exactly the most efficient of your team mates. You will find The Congenial deeply engaged in personal conversations as opposed to focusing on the task at hand. They are what I like to call emotional ADHD. They will pursue a sell without hesitation, only to be distracted by the conversation about sports, the kids, and current events, throwing to the wind the real reason why they clocked-in. Also, it is unfortunately not unusual to find partially completed work performed by The Congenial. Don't be surprised to find massive amounts of unfinished work left in

their wake. Finding a focused Congenial will truly benefit all those involved.

If your business or product will benefit from emotional attachment, if you find profitable or benefit from a community gathering like Floyd's Barbershop in the Andy Griffith show, then you need to hire a Congenial. The Congenial will have customers returning solely to see them, making purchases to satisfy them, and choosing your brand over the others because of your Congenial.

If you are an owner or if you are an executive over a department, it is your responsibility to be familiar with the image you want displayed firstly to your team. Your Customer Server will then adopt that image and display that image to your customers. The image being displayed to your customers will dictate the type of customer that will patronize your business. I've used this example earlier. Why do you think you prefer the Starbucks on the other side of town as opposed to the one right near you? Both are trained similarly, serving the same product. Most have the same decor. Why is it possible to prefer one over the other? Why is there just "something" different about one compared to the other? It is the image that is being displayed that fits your life style better. That image, again, started with the owner or department head that is so intimately involved and thus familiar with his business that he/she has styled a particular customer service or image those suites you better.

You need to find the image you want touted. The type of image will dictate the brand of customer service that is deployed. If you are trying to show your community that you are involved and that you care about the city's or town's growth, you certainly don't want your customer service to be stiff-shirt, unapproachable, overly elegant. You want your store to reflect a "green" environmentally friendly image. You would take care to decorate it in a way that your customers can clearly read or detect your message. Your Customer Server aid in that message, in that image display. Consequentially, a particular personality type fits one image better than the other. There's a lot more to having a service-based business than just opening your doors and hiring the cute college student to stand at your welcoming counter. Once you have nailed down the image you want to be your brand, hiring the first-rate Customer Server based upon that image will cause your business to sail on smooth waters. Until now you have been placing generic parts on the engine of your customer service. Discontinue the generic brand and use custom made engine material that was made just for your business.

Encouragements

Often in life we lose sight on what is important. All that involves obtaining, retaining, and maintaining success can obfuscate our vision on and pursuit for what should be considered vital. We have the tendency to disconnect as a result and attach to less important issues. Please understand your main focus or premise behind your pursuit will mold your business. It will create the face of your business. If your pursuit is founded in anything other than the facilitation and excellent delivery of genuine and memorable customer service, if customers and their experiences are not the fuel behind your pursuit, it will be more than noticeable to those who are looking. I don't care how large your company is, how long the company has been in existence, how financially comfortable the company is, non-customer oriented companies are as noticeable as the sun in a clear blue sky.

There's a reason why Amazon has appeared on 24/7 Wall St. top 5 best companies with excellent customer service list 7 years in a row, according to Douglass Mcintyre editor and CEO. There is a reason why Chic-fil-le ranked number one in 2016. Contrarily, there's no wonder why the two cable entertainment behemoths, Comcast and Dish Network, round out 24/7 Wall St.'s top ten Hall of Shame. We've all seen it. We've all experienced it. Your true mission in life as a business owner is apparent through your customer service.

So, in closing, I want to encourage you. I want to encourage you to refocus, to remove all distractions and obfuscations, to hone your vision once again on what is profoundly important.

Your Customers:

It doesn't matter how required your product is in the daily activities of mankind. The power to create success and destroy lies in the hand of the consumer. In 2015 Turing Pharmaceuticals, the maker of the drug Daraprim, used to treat life-threatening parasitic illnesses, increased their already incredibly high price from $13.50 to $750 a tablet. This increase caused uproar in the medical field. Doctors feared that because of the price increase they would have to opt for lesser expensive medication that would not treat the patient as well. The price hike, according to doctors, left patients vulnerable.

The outrage from doctors, patients, and other consumers was so resounding that it not only caused the owner of Turing Pharmaceuticals, Martin Shkreli, to dub himself "the most hated man on the internet," but it also caused his competition, Express Scripts Holding Co., to create the drug at a remarkably discounted price: $1.

I encourage you to remember that your customers are the most important part of your business. Catering to them in every way possible can do no harm. They are the bridge or portal to reach your desired aim and prosperity. Like a boxer's main focus should be his opponent, a fire fighter's should be the fire in front of him or her, yours is the customer. A Customer Server comes in different flavors: it comes in lawyer flavors, doctor flavors, banker flavors, pharmaceutical flavors, hotel manager flavors, restaurant owner flavors, and the list goes on and on. No matter the flavor, they are still Customer Servers. The facilitation of their services should not be self-centered but customer oriented. Their services should be developed in way to attract customers, to comfort customers. Too often business owners have the mindset that: "This is my tow truck service. Take it or leave it! I don't care how discomforted my services causes you to feel." Or "yes, I know you have an account with us. I'm going to force you to pay me extra to access your account" -- totally a self-centered way of dealing with their customers. This manner in which business owners present their product or service will most assuredly cause their business to collapse. Ask Turing Pharmaceutical.

You and Your Product of Service

What you do should have great significance and value. It is an expression of your talent, and extension to your identity. I used the example earlier how firm my mother was about my sister and my misbehaving in public, how she instilled in us that our conduct outside the walls of our home gave strangers an insight on the condition and the way in which things happened in our home. She wanted all to know that her social, moral, and cultural development should be considered advanced and by no means lacking.

Those of us serving the public must understand your product or service is performing the same actions. It is informing the public the extent to which you are developed. It you don't think this is true. Spend a night in a slummy hotel. Spend a week a dump apartment. Then, tell me what are your views or judgments of the owner of those facilities. You customers are drawing the same conclusions about your business based upon your customer service that accompanies your product or service.

I encourage you to value your business more, value the manner or style in which your product or service is being presented. Your Customer Servers are handlers of your precious creation. Your creation encapsulates your reputation. Why would you give you something of great importance to someone #1 unworthy, #2 unable to present you as profoundly respected within your particular sphere and profession? Hire no one short of stupendous to represent you and your product. Demand, expect, teach, and coach the utmost impactful customer service you can create for you and your product. It deserves it. You deserve it.

R

S

Our specialty is Customer Service Training and Staff Development geared toward all spheres of the service-based industry.

Our Customer Service Training is called "How To Be A Customer Server." Our approach to customer service involves not only the front line team members, but requires executives and department heads to participate.

It teaches all members of your team not just about the customer, it also involves metrics like Personality Placement, Strategic Hiring,Market Segment Training.

To schedule a How To Be A Customer Sever Learning Event visit our website: Sankofahospitality.weebly.com or call 815.683.8093.

For general speaking engagements, email sankofahospitality@gmail.com for calendar schedule.

Thank you,

Jeff

www.ingramcontent.com/pod-product-compliance
Lightning Source LLC
Chambersburg PA
CBHW060020210326
41520CB00009B/948